THE GREAT DINOSAUR MYSTERY SOLVED!

THE GREAT DINOSAUR MYSTERY SOLVED!

WRITTEN BY
KEN HAM

ILLUSTRATED BY
DAN LIETHA

Master
Books

Casebound edition
    First printing: April 1998
    Second printing: February 1999

Paperback edition
    First printing: April 2000
    Fourth printing, February 2004

ISBN: 0-89051-282-5
Library of Congress Number: 00-102595

Unless otherwise noted, all Scripture quoted is from the King James Version of the Bible.

Cover design by Dan Lietha

Printed in the United States of America

Please visit our website for other great titles:
www.masterbooks.net

For information regarding author interviews, please contact the publicity department at (870) 438-5288.

THANKS

I would like to express my sincere thanks to the following people who greatly contributed to the publication of this book:

R.L. David Jolly of Answers in Genesis for his many hours of research and invaluable help in obtaining the documentation in the extensive endnotes.

Dan Lietha of Answers in Genesis for using his talents in providing all of the illustrations.

Pastor Robert Ham (my brother) for writing the section entitled "WHAT IS A CHRISTIAN?"

TABLE OF CONTENTS

INTRODUCTION

*T*his is a unique approach to the topic of dinosaurs. It is not an exhaustive treatise on the fossils, behavior, or characteristics of dinosaurs. These subjects have been covered by numerous publications — many of which are referenced in the two appendices. These appendices, which are a great tool for students, teachers, and others, provide a wealth of information for those wishing to further research the topic of dinosaurs.

Appendix A consists of a massive collection of facts and theories about dinosaurs. This consists of quotes from or references to many different sources that give a good summary of current thinking and recent discoveries relating to dinosaurs. This is a great resource for students/ teachers/home schools etc., in researching and creating projects on dinosaurs.

Appendix B lists all the references used in collating the information given for each of the major illustrations in this book.

In this publication, I have attempted to demonstrate that when one takes the events of history as given in the Bible, as well as the doctrines of Christianity (that are all ultimately, directly or indirectly, founded in Genesis 1–11), that an entire WAY OF THINKING can actually be developed that can be applied to all areas of the created universe.

In other words, a true Christian philosophy STARTS with the time-line of history as given in Scripture. Once a person understands this, he or she will find it easy to be able to give many answers to a variety of questions, including dinosaurs.

Once you read through this book and understand its approach, you will be able to apply the same reasoning in other areas! You will be equipped to begin to give answers to questions that for many seem to be beyond their understanding. Try it! You'll be surprised by how much you really can say — once you believe and understand the Bible to be THE HISTORY BOOK OF THE UNIVERSE.

WHAT HAPPENED TO THE DINOSAURS?

WHY IS IT AN IMPORTANT QUESTION?

As far as most people are concerned, dinosaurs and evolution go hand in hand. Dinosaurs are used more than almost anything to convince children and adults alike that there have been millions of years of earth history. Most Christians do not know that the Bible can be used as a basis for explaining dinosaurs in terms of thousands of years of history, and solving the mystery of when they lived and what happened to them. After all, Colossians 2:3 states (about our Lord): "In whom are hid all the treasures of wisdom and knowledge."

> Bible Reading:
> Genesis 1:24–25
> Job 40:15–24

ARE DINOSAURS A MYSTERY?

Many think that the existence of dinosaurs and their demise is shrouded in such mystery that we may never know the truth about where they came from, when they lived, or what happened to them.

However, dinosaurs are only a mystery if you accept the evolutionary story of their history. According to evolutionists:

Dinosaurs first evolved around 235 million years ago,[1] long before man evolved (the Mesozoic Era is called the "dinosaur age"). No human being ever lived with dinosaurs, say evolutionists.

The record of their history is contained in the fossil layers over the earth that were deposited over millions of years. They were so successful as a group of animals, that dinosaurs eventually "ruled" the earth.

However, around *65 million years ago* something happened to change all of this — at the end of the Cretaceous period of the Mesozoic Era, dinosaurs died out. Most evolutionists believe some sort of cataclysmic event(s) destroyed them. One of the most popular theories about their extinction is that an asteroid hit the earth, resulting in a catastrophic change to the earth's climate and greatly affecting all life — especially the dinosaurs. However, many evolutionists claim that dinosaurs evolved into birds,[2] and thus they are not extinct, but are flying around us today. All these ideas are guesses and make dinosaurs a great mystery!

But, there is no mystery surrounding dinosaurs if you accept this totally different account of dinosaur history. According to biblical history:

Dinosaurs first existed around 6,000 years ago.[3] Because dinosaurs were land animals, and God made all the land animals on day six of the creation week,[4, 5] dinosaurs were created on day six.

Dinosaurs could not have died out before this time because death, bloodshed, disease, and suffering is a result of Adam's sin.[6]

Adam and Eve were also made on day six alongside the dinosaurs — so dinosaurs lived with people. Representatives of all the KINDS of land animals, including the dinosaur kinds went on board Noah's ark. All those that were left behind drowned in the cataclysmic circumstances of the flood — many of their remains became fossils.

After the flood (around 4,500 years ago), the land animals (including dinosaurs) came off the ark and lived in the present world, beside people. Because of sin, the judgment of the curse and the effects of the flood have greatly changed the earth. Since the flood, many animals have died out from diseases, a lack of food, etc. The dinosaurs, like many other creatures, seem to have also died out. According to this view, there is no mystery about dinosaurs!

WHY ARE THE TWO VIEWS SO DIFFERENT?

Where wast thou when I laid the foundations of the earth? declare, if thou hast understanding (Job 38:4).

*H*ow can there be such totally different explanations for dinosaurs? Think about this — whether one is an evolutionist or accepts the Bible's account of history, all the evidence for dinosaurs is the same. All scientists have the same facts — they have the same world, the same fossils, the same living creatures, and the same universe.

If the "facts" are all the same, then how
can the explanations be so different?

The reason is quite simple. Scientists only have the present to work with — dinosaur fossils only exist in the present. Yet scientists try to connect the fossils they find to the past. They ask: "What happened in history to bring dinosaurs into existence and form their fossils, and cause them not to be around today?"[7]

Obviously, no scientist has lived through all the history of the earth. There is no way to explain dinosaurs, unless someone (who can be trusted) has recorded the events of history to enable us to explain the evidence we now see before us.

Thus, real science, using our five senses in the present, cannot ultimately answer questions about the unobservable and unreported past! Real science can build jet airplanes, make computers, and so on — but real (observational) science cannot deal directly with the past, as we work only in the present. Most people don't realize that evolution is not science — it's a belief about the past.

Creation is not science, either — it's a belief about the past based on the record in the Bible that itself claims

to be the Word of God, of one who has always existed,[8] and who is perfect and never tells a lie.[9] The Bible claims to be a true record of history — past and future.

Many people think the Bible is just a book about religion or salvation. But in essence, it is much more than this. The Bible is THE HISTORY BOOK OF THE UNIVERSE from the very beginning. It gives us an account of when time began (Gen. 1:1), and the events of history such as the entrance of sin and death into the world — the time when the WHOLE world (globe) was destroyed by water — the giving of different languages at the Tower of Babel — the account of the Son of God coming as man, and His death and resurrection — and the new heaven and earth to come.

Ultimately there are only two ways of thinking — one that starts with the revelation (biblical record) from God as foundational to ALL thinking (biology, history, geology, etc.) — which would be called a CHRISTIAN WORLD VIEW; or, starting with man's beliefs (evolutionary history) as foundational to ALL thinking — which would be called a SECULAR WORLD VIEW.

Most Christians have been indoctrinated through the media and education system to think in a secular way. They tend to take their secular thinking TO the Bible, instead of using the Bible to BUILD all their thinking.

If one begins by accepting the evolutionist view of history that has no written record or eyewitnesses, then an entire way of thinking based upon this view will be used to explain the evidence that exists in the present. Thus, the evolutionist explanation of dinosaurs given above.

The History Book of the Universe!

The Holy Bible

But if one begins by accepting the biblical view of history from the written record of an eyewitness to all events of history, then a totally different way of thinking will be used to explain the SAME evidence. Thus, the biblical explanation of dinosaurs given on page 13.

WHICH VIEW IS RIGHT?

*The fear of the Lord is the beginning
of wisdom* (Prov. 9:10).

*The fear of the Lord is the beginning
of knowledge* (Prov. 1:7).

*M*any Christians do not know how to deal with dinosaurs. The main reason is because they are not using the Bible as their book of history. In other words, they are not building their framework of thinking on the events of history as recorded in the Bible.

For instance, if the Bible teaches there was no death of animals or people before the fall of Adam, then this will affect the way Christians interpret fossils. Also, if there really was a global flood, this will have a direct bearing on a Christian view of geologic history. In addition, if all land animals were made directly by God on the same day as people, this will affect how a person interprets the history of dinosaurs, and so on.

In fact, the purpose of this book is to show that when one does start WITH the Bible to build a framework of thinking, one can consistently interpret the evidence concerning dinosaurs and construct a history that can be logically defended. Biblical history does make sense of the evidence, even if one doesn't know much about dinosaurs. By starting with the Bible, LOTS can be explained about dinosaurs.

At the same time, we will reveal that the evolutionist view of history cannot consistently explain the evidence or be logically defended.

DINOSAUR HISTORY

HOW DO WE KNOW DINOSAURS EVER EXISTED?

Fossil bones of what are now called dinosaurs are found all over the world. Although many finds consist of just fragments of bones,[10] some remarkable discoveries of nearly complete skeletons have been found. Scientists have been able to describe many different types of animals that fit under the heading "dinosaurs," based on distinctive characteristics such as the structure of the skull, limbs, etc. However, there doesn't appear to be any consistent definition as to what is or what is not a dinosaur.[11]

Evolutionists claim that these bones date back millions of years. But it's important to realize that when they dig up a dinosaur bone, it doesn't have any label attached to it showing its date! Evolutionists obtain their dates by INDIRECT dating methods that other scientists show cannot even be trusted.[12]

There is also evidence that evolutionists cannot ignore which indicates dinosaur bones are not that old. Scientists at the University of Montana found *T. rex* bones that were not totally fossilized! The sections of the bones

that were like fresh bone also contained what seemed to be blood cells.[13] If these bones really were millions of years old, then the blood cells would have already totally disintegrated. Also, there shouldn't be "fresh" bone if it is really millions of years old.[14] A report by these scientists stated the following:

"A thin slice of *T. rex* bone glowed amber beneath the lens of my microscope . . . the lab filled with murmurs of amazement, for I had focused on something inside the vessels that none of us had ever noticed before: tiny round objects, translucent red with a dark center . . . red blood cells? The shape and location suggested them, but blood cells are mostly water and couldn't possibly have stayed preserved in the 65-million-year-old tyrannosaur."

"The bone sample that had us so excited came from a beautiful, nearly complete specimen of *Tyrannosaurus rex* unearthed in 1990. . . . When the team brought the dinosaur into the lab, we noticed that some parts deep inside the long bone of the leg had not completely fossilized. . . . So far, we think that all of this evidence supports the notion that our slices of *T. rex* could contain preserved heme as hemoglobin fragments. But more work needs to be done before we are confident enough to come right out and say, 'Yes, this *T. rex* has blood compounds left in its tissues.' "[15]

"In another effort to make fossils speak in new ways, post-graduate student Mary Schweitzer has been trying to extract DNA from the bones of *T. rex*. Originally, like Kristi, she had intended to thin-section the bones and conduct a histologic investigation. But under the microscope there appeared to be blood cells preserved within the bone tissue. Mary conducted a number of tests in an attempt to rule out the possibility that what she'd

discovered were in fact blood cells. The tests instead confirmed her initial interpretation."[16]

Also, a creation scientist found "fresh" frozen dinosaur bones in Alaska.[17] Now, even evolutionists would not argue that this deposit of bones had stayed frozen for the many millions of years since these dinosaurs supposedly died out (according to evolutionary theory). The bones were not fossilized. They should not be in this state if they really were millions of years old. From a biblical perspective, there was no death, bloodshed, disease,[18] or suffering before sin.[19] If one takes Genesis to Revelation consistently, interpreting Scripture with Scripture, then death and bloodshed of man and animals came into the world only *after* Adam sinned. The first death of an animal occurred when God shed an animal's blood in the garden and clothed Adam and Eve (Gen. 3:21). This was also a picture of the atonement — symbolic of Christ's blood that was needed to be shed for us.

Thus, from a theological perspective, there could NOT have been any dead or diseased bones of dinosaurs or any animal before sin — this would undermine the entire gospel. For the origin of the dinosaur bones to be explained from a biblical framework, the dinosaurs had to have died only *after* sin entered the world, not before. This means these bones could NOT be millions of years old. This fits with the fact that the biblical age of the earth (using a literal chronology of the Bible) dates to only thousands of years, not millions.

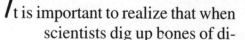

WHAT DID DINOSAURS LOOK LIKE?

It is important to realize that when scientists dig up bones of dinosaurs, they do not uncover an animal with its flesh still intact. Even if they found *all* the bones (and they often have only a few fragments), scientists still would have less than 40 percent of the animal to tell them what it originally looked like. For example, the bones do not tell the color of the animal, or what it ate for dinner. Even though some fossils of skin impressions have been found,[20] when scientists reconstruct dinosaurs from bony remains, they have had to make all kinds of assumptions.

Sometimes scientists have made mistakes in their reconstructions, which have had to be corrected when additional bones and other evidence were found. For instance, the famous *Brontosaurus* is no longer in dinosaur dictionaries: the original discoverer put the wrong head on a skeleton of a dinosaur that had already been named.[21] Because there is some diversity of color among reptiles living today, it is valid to assume dinosaurs may have greatly varied in color, skin texture, and so on. In the final analysis there is much speculation in this area.

WHERE DID DINOSAURS COME FROM AND WHEN DID THEY LIVE?

Evolutionists guess that dinosaurs evolved from some reptile that had itself originally evolved from amphibians. However, they can't point to any transitional forms (i.e., in between) to substantiate their argument. If one looks up a dinosaur family tree in an evolutionist book, it will show many distinct types of dinosaurs, but only hypothetical lines joining them up to some common ancestor.[22] Evolutionists simply cannot defend their interpretation of the evidence.

The biblical record in Genesis states that God made all things in six days (the Hebrew word for day in Genesis 1, *yom*, as used here with a number and the phrase

THE DAYS OF CREATION IN GENESIS ONE!

DAY 1 — EARTH, SPACE, TIME & LIGHT

DAY 2 — ATMOSPHERE

DAY 3 — DRY LAND & PLANTS

DAY 4 — SUN, MOON & STARS

DAY 5 — SEA & FLYING CREATURES

DAY 6 — LAND ANIMALS & MAN

"evening and morning" means an ordinary solar day).[23]

On day six, God made all the kinds of land animals (Gen. 1:24–25). Because dinosaurs were land animals, they must have been made on this day, around 6,000 years ago[24] (the approximate date of creation obtained from adding up all the years in the Bible).

God also gave Adam and Eve dominion over the animals: "And God blessed them, and God said unto them, Be fruitful, and multiply, and replenish the earth, and subdue it: and have dominion over the fish of the sea, and over the fowl of the air, and over every living thing that moveth upon the earth" (Gen. 1:28). But looking at today's world we are reminded of Hebrews 2:8: "Thou hast put all things in subjection under his feet. For in that he put all in subjection under him, he left nothing that is not put under him. But now we see not yet all things put under him." You see, man's relationship with all things changed because of sin, as we will see later.

QUESTION: DOES GOD TELL US WHEN HE MADE TYRANNOSAURUS REX?

*M*any Christians would say no. But if *T. rex* was a land animal, and God made all the land animals on day six, then God made *T. rex* on day six! The point is, when we build our thinking on the Bible, we have a way of thinking that enables us to give answers about the evidence we have around us.

T. rex skull

Tyrannosaurus rex [tie-RAN-oh-SAWR-us],
meaning "tyrant lizard king," belongs to the Class: Reptilia;
Infraclass: Archosauromorpha; Superorder: Archosauria; Order:
Saurischia (lizard-hipped dinosaur); Suborder: Theropoda;
Infraorder: Carnosauria; Family: Tyrannosauridae.

TYRANNOSAURUS REX

Tyrannosaurus was among the largest of all land carnivores,
measuring up to 40 feet in length, standing 20 feet tall, and
weighing an estimated 8 U.S. tons. The skull is up to 5 feet in
length and contains 6- to 8-inch long teeth equipped with
serrated edges. With such teeth, evolutionary scientists are
quick to see an animal that was a ferocious meat-eater.
However, we know that originally *T. rex* was a vegetarian:

Genesis 1: 30 states, "And to every beast of the earth, and to every fowl of the air, and to every thing that creepeth upon the earth, wherein there is life, I have given every green herb for meat and it was so." It's certainly possible that *T. rex* teeth were designed for eating special types of "green herb" such as large melons, gourds, coconuts, and large hard seed pods (or even tree and fern branches), to name a few possibilities. It's also conceivable that the Curse might have resulted in changes to their structure, either degenerative or by deliberate design.

Another characteristic includes a short neck made of very thick vertebrae to support the head. Sizable spines on the neck vertebrae indicate the attachment of large powerful muscles which would have been needed to support such a large head.

Other large powerful muscles were found on the rather long ribs. These muscles may have also been used for the support and movement of the neck and head. The ilium or upper pelvic bone, with its large blade shape, contained a rather complex pattern of rough edges and ridges, which indicated where the sacral ribs of the backbone attached. A number of bones around the hip joint are fused together, forming a solid bar of bone that bore the weight and stress of the entire animal.

The bones of the hind legs are huge and exceptionally strong, and end with broad feet bearing three toes forward and a spur-like first toe in the rear. There is some controversy as to how fast the *Tyrannosaurus* could run. One strength-indicator test conducted on the femur revealed a strength indicator of only 9 units, which indicates that it could not have been very fast, contrary to movie depictions of a sprinting *T. rex*. By comparison, a female African elephant on the same test shows a strength indicator of 6-14 units.

Another characteristic of *Tyrannosaurus* is the two very small forearms which could seem to reach neither the ground nor its mouth. While the shoulder girdle is large and indicates powerful muscle attachment, the forearms are surprisingly small with two fingers and claws. Scientists have speculated on the function of these tiny arms, but until we find the record of someone who actually observed them in use, we may never know.

Tyrannosaurus was created on day six of the creation week as revealed in Genesis 1:25, "And God made the beast of the earth after his kind, and cattle after their kind, and every thing that creepeth upon the earth after his kind: and God saw that it was good." It was rediscovered (remember, Adam "discovered" the first dinosaurs) in 1900 by Barnum Brown in western Wyoming. Brown found the lower jaw and backbone of what appeared to be a very large carnivore. The specimen was named *Dynamosaurus imperiousus* ("imperial powerful lizard") by Brown's boss, Henry Fairfield Osborn, then director of the vertebrate paleontology department at the American Museum. Osborn eventually changed the name to *Tyrannosaurus rex* in 1906. This specimen can be seen on display at the British Museum of Natural History in London.

Brown made a trip to the Hell Creek region of eastern Montana in 1902, after looking at a piece of fossil and photos taken several years before by a friend while hunting deer. As soon as Brown arrived at the Sieber Ranch site in Garfield County, he found a bit of bone, the color of "milky coffee" in the "flinty blue sandstone." He spent the next three years excavating the pelvic girdle, hind limbs, and backbones. In 1905, while Brown was still excavating the specimen, Henry Fairfield Osborn named the specimen *Tyrannosaurus rex*, stating:

"I propose to make this animal the type of the new genus, *Tyrannosaurus*, in reference to its size, which greatly exceeds that of any carnivorous land animal hitherto described." Osborn then added *rex* as the species name, making the new find the "tyrant lizard king". Osborn celebrated the new museum specimen, measuring 39 feet long and 19 feet tall, saying, "This animal is in fact the *ne plus ultra* of the evolution of the large carnivorous dinosaurs: in brief it is entitled to the royal and high sounding name which I have applied to it." (At the time, Osborn also wrote that the *Tyrannosaurus* was only three or four million years old.)

This *Tyrannosaurus* is about 50 percent complete and can be seen on display at the Carnegie Museum in Pittsburgh, Pennsylvania. The American Museum of Natural History sold the type specimen to the Carnegie Museum during World War II, fearing that Nazi Germany might bomb New York City.

A 90 percent complete *T. rex* skeleton was found in 1988 by Kathy Wankel in McCone County, Montana. In 1990 a crew from the Montana State University's Museum of the Rockies excavated the nearly complete skeleton. It has been on display at the Museum in Bozeman, Montana, while it has been going through preparation. This is the specimen in which Mary Schweitzer of Montana State University found the red blood cells in the partially unfossilized femur. These red blood cells provide excellent evidence that these fossils are not millions of years old, but are no more than a few thousand years old.

The 11th *T. rex* found is probably the most famous. On August 12, 1990, Sue Hendrickson of the Black Hills Institute in South Dakota found the *T. rex* and so it was named "Sue" after her. "Sue" is nearly 90 percent complete and the largest *T. rex* ever found, measuring 40 feet long and standing 20 feet tall, including a 5-foot-long skull.

Pete Larson of the Black Hills School paid the Sioux landowner $5,000 for the rights to excavate the site located on the Cheyenne River Sioux Reservation. The leaders of the reservation requested that the assistant U.S. attorney in Pierre, South Dakota, investigate Larson's collection of the fossil. The U.S. attorney ruled that Larson had violated the Federal Antiquities Act, which "prohibits outsiders from making contracts with people of the Indian community without federal permission." Sue was subsequently confiscated by the Federal Bureau of Investigation (FBI) and impounded in a warehouse at the South Dakota School of Mines. The ownership of Sue was disputed in court, but was finally placed on the auction block. On October 4, 1997, Chicago's Field Museum of Natural History spent seven minutes of auction time in purchasing the fossil for an incredible total sum of $8,362,500.

Another interesting aspect of "Sue" is her history of disease and injury. Though her skeleton is considered to be in prime condition, there was evidence of a broken and healed left fibula, ribs, and tail bones. It also had evidence of bite and puncture marks on the left side of the skull and signs of muscle re-attachment on the right humerus. These injuries must have occurred after the fall (the entrance of sin, bloodshed, and death) as God in Genesis 1:31 declared all of creation was very good at the end of the sixth day: "And God saw every thing that he had made, and, behold, it was very good. And the evening and the morning were the sixth day."

There have been a few more recent finds of *T. rex* in Texas and possibly Mongolia but all of these finds have been large adults. The discovery of younger *T. rex* can be summed up in the words of the famous paleontologist John Horner, "But no one has ever found more than one reasonably complete T. rex at a time. No one has ever found the skeleton of a young *T. rex*, or a definite *T. rex* footprint, *T. rex* nest, or *T. rex* egg. And we're lucky to have the II *T. rexes* we've got." (Horner & Lessem. 1993. p. 17)

See Appendix B for references used for collating this information.

WHO DISCOVERED DINOSAURS?

$\mathcal{S}$ecular books would tell you that the first discovery of what later were called dinosaurs was in 1677 when Dr. Robert Plot found bones so big they were thought to belong to a giant elephant or giant human.[25] In 1763, Brooks

used the name *Scrotum humanum* to caption the drawing of the bone that Plot had found.[26]

In 1822, Mary Anne Mantell went for a walk along a country road in Sussex. According to tradition, she found a stone which glittered in the sunlight and took it home to show her fossil-collecting husband. Dr. Mantell noticed that the stone contained a tooth similar to, but much larger than, that of modern reptiles. He concluded that it belonged to some extinct giant plant-eating reptile with teeth like an iguana. In 1825 he named the owner of the tooth *Iguanodon* (Iguana tooth).[27] It was Dr. Mantell who began to popularize the age of reptiles.[28]

From a biblical perspective, however, the above discoveries were actually when dinosaurs were *rediscovered!* The first time dinosaurs were "discovered" was when Adam saw the kinds of land animals God had created on the sixth day of creation — because dinosaurs were land animals, the sixth day must have included the creation of the dinosaur kinds (Gen. 1:24–25).

DINOSAURS WITH PEOPLE?

*E*volutionists are dogmatic that dinosaurs never lived beside humans — these creatures supposedly died out millions of years before man evolved![29] But, in fact, there is a lot of historical evidence that dinosaurs

did live with humans. This will be discussed in detail later.

Because the Bible teaches that the animals we now call dinosaurs were made on the same day as the first two people (Gen. 1:24–31), Christians can authoritatively state that dinosaurs did live with people! This can be declared on the basis of the authority of the Word of God. This is thinking biblically!

WHERE DID THE WORD 'DINOSAUR' COME FROM?

The King James Bible was first translated in 1611. Some people think that because the word "dinosaur" is not found in this or other translations, then the Bible makes no mention of dinosaurs.

However, it wasn't until 1841 that the word "dinosaur" was first coined![30] Sir Richard Owen, a famous British anatomist, and first superintendent of the British Museum[31] at age 38, originated the word, from two Greek words, *deinos* and *sauros*, which means "terrible lizard."[32] After viewing the bones of *Iguanodon* and *Megalosaurus*, he realized he was examining the remains of a unique group of reptiles that had not yet been classified as such before.

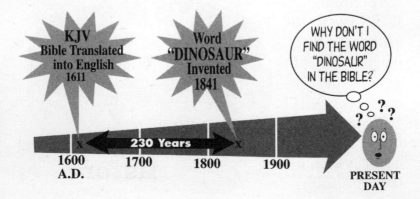

*Thus, one would not expect to find the
word "dinosaur" in the Bible!*

But the word dinosaur and its meaning of "terrible
lizard" has helped popularize the idea that all dinosaurs
were enormous and savage monsters! We shall find out
that this is far from true. Had Richard Owen known about
the REST of the dinosaurs, he may never have coined
the word!

Is There Another Word for Dinosaur?

We've all heard of the word "dragon." Dragon legends are
numerous around the world. Legends tell us that the Chinese bred dragons.[33] Many of the descriptions of these "dragons" fit dinosaurs. Could the stories about dragons actually
be accounts of encounters with what we now call dinosaurs?

**Dragons:
Dinosaurs in History**

Dragon

The dragon pictured here is actually based on a dinosaur called Baryonyx walkeri [bar-ee-ON-icks] which means "heavy claw." Class: Reptilia; Infraclass: Archosauromorpha; Superorder: Archosauria; Order: Saurischia (lizard-hipped dinosaurs); Suborder: Theropoda; Infraorder: Tetanurae or Coelurosauria (depending on reference); Superfamily: Spinosauroidea; Family: Baryonychidae.

THE DRAGON

Dragons have long been thought of as creatures of mere legend. Actually, they were real creatures that lived with many of the animals we see today and with man. The Bible talks about dragons as real animals as we read in Psalm 91:13, "Thou shalt tread upon the lion and adder: the young lion and the dragon shalt thou trample under feet."

Isaiah 43:20 also speaks of dragons as real animals, "The beast of the field shall honor me, the dragons and the owls: because I give waters in the wilderness, [and] rivers in the desert, to give drink to my people, my chosen." In both of these Scriptures, the use of the word dragon is coupled with other real animals in a way that illustrates that the author knew of these creatures.

Baryonyx was up to 34 feet in length, 10 to 13 feet in height, and weighed two U.S. tons. There is some controversy as to whether *Baryonyx* walked on two feet or on four.

Baryonyx was rediscovered in 1983 by an amateur fossil hunter by the name of William Walker who was fossil hunting in a clay pit in Sussex, England. He found a huge curved claw that measured 12 inches, hence the name *Baryonyx*, "heavy claw." By 1986 paleontologists A.J. Charig and A.C. Milner, from the Natural History Museum in London, identified the find as belonging to a previously unknown species of dinosaur and thus gave it the *name Baryonyx walkeri*; Greek βαρυ, "heavy," "strong"; ονυξ, "talon," "claw"; and *walkeri* in honor of William Walker its founder. The announcement was made in an article in *Nature* and was billed by some as one of the most important European dinosaur discoveries of this century.

After the discovery of the claw, a team of paleontologists from the Natural History Museum in London spent three weeks excavating the site. Some of the bones they found were loose in the clay; the majority of the skeleton was found in hard blocks of iron-impregnated siltstone. Before the bones' removal, the entire site, including each bone and rock slab, was carefully mapped out. Then the bones and rock slabs were carefully wrapped and shipped back to the museum where scientists used a shot-blaster, power chisels, and diamond-bladed saws to remove the excess rock. As the bones were exposed, they were covered with a protective coating of resin to prevent damage. The final layers of matrix were then removed by scientists working under a stereo microscope.

Before the skeleton was assembled, scientists began to model the missing pieces of the skeleton and made casts of the bones they did have. The models were made out of softened wax or modeling clay. The casts were made by first making a mold of the bone, using silicone rubber. Then a bone-colored resin and fiberglass were used to make exact replicas of the original bones. These replicas are often used to study the bones instead of the originals which are fragile and easily damaged.

The *Baryonyx* skeleton was only about 60 percent complete, so as they assembled the skeleton, they had to use nearly 40 percent fabricated pieces. Since the huge claw was not found attached to the skeleton, it was unsure if it went on the forelimbs or hind limbs. It is generally thought that it must have been carried on the forelimbs, since it would have been awkward for the dinosaur to have wielded it from a hind limb; also the forelimbs were unusually thick and powerfully built and would have easily wielded such a claw.

Another unique feature of *Baryonyx* is its skull. The skull is long and narrow and the jaw has an s-shaped curve that resembles that of the modern crocodile. It had a large number of small pointed teeth, (32 teeth per jaw ramus but only 16 larger teeth in the upper jaw), twice as many as other dinosaurs that were considered meat-eaters. The skull also had a shallow nasal crest on the top.

With its unusual jaw, and with a neck that was not as flexible as most other theropods, and a huge claw, *Baryonyx* proves to be somewhat of a mystery for the scientists. The general current theory is that *Baryonyx* was a fish-eater (as possibly indicated by the large number of small pointed teeth) and that it would use its huge claw to hook and snag fish from a river or shallow waters, much like a grizzly bear does. This idea was supported when fossil scales and teeth of a fish, *Lepidotes*, were found in the area where the stomach would have been (of course, the pre-Fall diet of *Baryonyx* would have been vegetation, as stated in Genesis 1:30).

Baryonyx is on display at the Natural History Museum in London. If you ever get the chance to view this wonderful specimen, remember that you just might be looking at the skeleton of one of the dragons from English history and legend (e.g., Sir George the Dragon Slayer) or one of the dragons spoken of in the Bible. One can easily understand how people could embellish the features of a dinosaur like *Baryonyx* over the years, adding fanciful appendages, etc., to result in some of the dragon pictures and sculptures that have come down to us today.

See Appendix B for references used for collating this information.

In a glass case in the British Museum in London lies one of the oldest books of British history — *The Anglo-Saxon Chronicles*. This book records encounters people had with

The Flag of Wales

dragons, and many of the descriptions fit well-known dinosaurs.[34] In fact, the emblem on the flag of the country of Wales is a dragon.

In the film, *The Great Dinosaur Mystery*[35], a number of dragon legends are recounted:

A Sumerian story dating back to 3000 B.C. tells of a hero named Gilgamesh, who, when he went to fell cedars in a remote forest, encountered a huge vicious dragon which he slew, cutting off its head as a trophy.

China has always been renowned for its dragon stories, and dragons have always been prominent on Chinese pottery, embroidery, and carvings.

England has its story of St. George, who slew a dragon that lived in a cave.

There is the story of a tenth-century Irishman who wrote of his encounter of what appears to have been a *Stegosaurus*.

In the 1500s, a European scientific book, *Historia Animalium*, listed several animals, which to us are dinosaurs, as still alive. A well-known naturalist of the time, Ulysses Aldrovandus, recorded an encounter between a peasant named

Baptista and a dragon whose description fits that of the dinosaur *Tanystropheus*. The encounter was on May 13, 1572, near Bologna in Italy, and the peasant killed the dragon.

See Appendix A at the end of this book for references used for collating this information.

It is highly interesting to note that the word "dragon" (Hebrew: *tannim*) appears in the Old Testament at least 21 times.[36] If one replaces "dragon" with "dinosaur," it fits very nicely in the biblical text.[37]

There are passages in the Bible about dragons that lived on the land:

. . . the dragons of the wilderness (Mal. 1:3).
. . . they snuffed up the wind like dragons (Jer. 14:6).

Biblical creationists believe these were references to what we now call dinosaurs. There are also passages in the Bible about dragons that lived in the sea.

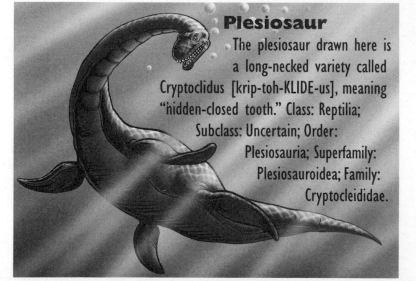

Plesiosaur
The plesiosaur drawn here is a long-necked variety called Cryptoclidus [krip-toh-KLIDE-us], meaning "hidden-closed tooth." Class: Reptilia; Subclass: Uncertain; Order: Plesiosauria; Superfamily: Plesiosauroidea; Family: Cryptocleididae.

PLESIOSAUR

Plesiosaurs [plee-zee-OH-sores] were created on day five of the creation week along with the rest of the creatures of the sea as we read in Genesis 1:20–23, "And God said, Let the waters bring forth abundantly the moving creature that hath life, and fowl that may fly above the earth in the open firmament of heaven. And God created great whales, and every living creature that moveth, which the waters brought forth abundantly, after their kind, and every winged fowl after his kind: and God saw that it was good. And God blessed them, saying, be fruitful, and multiply, and fill the waters in the seas, and let fowl multiply in the earth. And the evening and the morning were the fifth day."

Plesiosaurs were a group of marine-dwelling reptiles (they were not true dinosaurs), that ranged in size from the 7-foot-long *Plesiosaurus* to the 46-foot-long *Elasmosaurus*. *Plesiosaurs* had deep bodies, short tails, and more than the normal five bones in each finger on their flipper (they often had as many as ten bones in each finger). *Plesiosaurs* also had a unique structuring for their flippers that no other group of marine reptiles had. The collarbones and two of the three hip bones were very large and formed broad plates on the underside of the body. They were used for the attachments of the powerful muscles and for swimming. These bone plates were connected by a dense series of ventral ribs, making the body more rigid and providing strong support structure against which the large flippers could work. Since most paleontologists believe that *plesiosaurs* crawled up on the beach to lay their eggs (in similar fashion to sea turtles), the bone plates and rib structures would also have provided the necessary support and protection for this.

Plesiosaurs are divided into two groups or superfamilies: those with short necks and large heads, such as *Kronosaurus* (depicted in this book as *Leviathan*), which are in the superfamily *Pliosauroidea*; and those with long necks and small heads, such as *Cryptoclidus* shown here, which are in the superfamily *Plesiosauroidea*.

Cryptoclidus was rediscovered in Peterborough, England, and named by H.G. Seeley in 1892. It is about 13 feet long with 35 vertebrae in the neck, which suggests great flexibility for grasping at small fish and other invertebrates for its post-Fall diet. *Cryptoclidus* had a large number of small, pointed teeth that curved back and overlapped when the mouth was closed. Evolutionary scientists think that these teeth would have worked well for grabbing mouthfuls of small fish, shrimp, or ammonites, straining the water out through the net of teeth. However, we know that before the Fall, creatures ate plants and herbs; therefore these teeth would have been very effective for eating different forms of kelp and algae and could have even worked like a garden rake to help in the harvesting of these plants. The skull and lower jaw suggests that *Cryptoclidus* had powerful jaw muscles.

Originally, scientists thought that *plesiosaurs* swam by rowing themselves through the water with a front to back motion of their flippers. Upon closer examination of the skeletons, it is now believed that they would "fly" through the water, using their front flippers in a flying motion in the manner of penguins and sea turtles, using their back flippers for steering and stabilization.

Since none of the creatures of the sea were taken on Noah's ark, there would be a strong possibility that some *plesiosaurs* and maybe even some *ichthyosaurs* survived the flood. The violent and turbulent waters of the flood would surely have killed and buried many of the sea creatures (over 90 percent of fossils found are of marine animals). However, if some had survived the flood and lived on in the seas for years after, they could help account for many of the legends of sea monsters that have been gathered from all over the world. Remote as it may seem, there could even be the possibility that a few have survived till modern times. After all, it's much easier to believe that they could have survived for several thousand years rather than for nearly a hundred-million years.

See Appendix B for references used for collating this information.

> *. . . thou brakest the heads of the dragons in the waters* (Ps. 74:13).

> *. . . and he shall slay the dragon that is in the sea* (Isa. 27:1).

Even though the word "dinosaur" refers, technically speaking, to animals that lived on the land, many people group the sea reptiles and flying reptiles with dinosaurs. We could argue that the dragons that lived in

Tylosaur Skeleton

the water were probably dinosaur-like animals such as the *Plesiosaurus*.

Job 41 has a description of a great animal that lived in the sea, *Leviathan*, that even breathed fire. This "dragon" may have been something like the mighty *Kronosaurus*.[38]

Leviathan The Leviathan pictured here is an adaptation of the large marine reptile known as Kronosaurus queenslandicus, which means "Time Reptile." Class: Reptilia; Subclass: Uncertain; Order: Plesiosauria; Superfamily: Pliosauroidea; Family: Dolichorhynchopidae or Pliosauridae (depending upon reference).

LEVIATHAN

The *Leviathan* [leh-VI-a-than] is described in Job 41:1–34, "Canst thou draw out leviathan with an hook? Or his tongue with a cord which thou lettest down? Canst thou put an hook into his nose? Or bore his jaw through with a thorn?

Will he make many supplications unto thee? Will he speak soft words unto thee? Will he make a covenant with thee? Wilt thou take him for a servant for ever? Wilt thou play with him as with a bird? Or wilt thou bind him for thy maidens?

Shall the companions make a banquet of him? Shall they part him among the merchants? Canst thou fill his skin with barbed irons? Or his head with fish spears? Lay thine hand upon him, remember the battle, do no more.

Behold, the hope of him is in vain: shall not one be cast down even at the sight of him? None is so fierce that dare stir him up: who then is able to stand before me? Who hath prevented me, that I should repay him? Whatsoever is under the whole heaven is mine.

I will not conceal his parts, nor his power, nor his comely proportion. Who can discover the face of his garment? Or who can come to him with double bridle? Who can open the doors of his face? His teeth are terrible round about.

His scales are his pride, shut up together as with a close seal. One is so near to another, that no air can come between them. They are joined one to another, they stick together, that they cannot be sundered.

By his neesings a light doth shine, and his eyes are like the eyelids of the morning. Out of his mouth go burning lamps, and sparks of fire leap out. Out of his nostrils goeth smoke, as out of a seething pot or caldron. His breath kindleth coals, and a flame goeth out of his mouth. In his neck remaineth strength, and sorrow is turned into joy before him. The flakes of his flesh are joined together: they are firm in themselves; they cannot be moved. His heart is as firm as a stone; yea, as hard as a piece of the nether millstone.

When he raiseth up himself, the mighty are afraid: by reason of breakings they purify themselves. The sword of him that layeth at him cannot hold: the spear, the dart, not the habergeon. He esteemeth iron as straw, and brass as rotten wood.

The arrow cannot make him flee: slingstones are turned with him into stubble. Darts are counted as stubble: he laugheth at the shaking of a spear. Sharp stones are under him: he spreadeth sharp pointed things upon the mire.

He maketh the deep to boil like a pot: he maketh the sea like a pot of ointment. He maketh a path to shine after him; one would think the deep to be hoary. Upon the earth there is not his like, who is made without fear.

He beholdeth all high things: he is a king over all the children of pride."

Kronosaurus measured over 42 feet in length and, according to one author, "Its skull was flat-topped and massively long, measuring 9 feet/2.7m — almost a quarter of the total body length, and therefore substantially larger and more powerful than that of the greatest carnivorous dinosaur, *Tyrannosaurus.*" (Dixon. p. 77)

Kronosaurus was rediscovered in 1899 by A. Crombie, near Hughenden, Queensland, Australia. Crombie found a fragment of the jaw that held six teeth. A Dr. Longman, then director of the Australian Museum, described the animal as an *ichthyosaur* and named it *Kronosaurus queenslandicus.* It wasn't until more fragments were located and examined that Dr. Longman changed his classification of it to the short-necked *plesiosaur* group known as *pliosaurs.*

The best specimen was found in 1931, north of Richmond, Australia, in an area dominated by limestone. A group from Harvard University's Museum of Comparative Zoology worked on excavating the fossil from 1931 to 1932 and then shipped it to the museum in the United States for three years of preparation. This *Kronosaurus* measures 42 feet/12.8m in length with a skull measuring 9 feet/2.7m and is nearly complete except for some missing parts of the fore flippers and the end of the tail. It is still on display at the Museum of Comparative Zoology at Harvard University.

Interestingly, this specimen was taken to the Harvard Museum (USA) without a license from the Australian government and without any involvement from Australian scientists or institutions. This has not set well with the scientific community in Australia and if any further specimens of *Kronosaurus* are found, they will most likely remain in Australia.

Kronosaurus was considered to be a powerful swimmer and

highly maneuverable, allowing it to feed on fish, other marine reptiles, and the abundance of invertebrates such as ammonites. The front teeth of Kronosaurus were very sharp and pointed, but the rear teeth were more rounded, making it quite easy to crush the shells of the ammonites and other invertebrates. These teeth would also have been well-designed to feed on a variety of kelps and sea grasses before the Fall.

It has long been thought that the largest of the marine reptiles were Kronosaurus and an icthyosaur called Shonixaurus, both of which were the same length as the largest of the toothed whales, the sperm whale. However, historical records from Oxford Clay have indicated that an even larger pliosaur existed. Comparisons between the cervical vertebrae and Kronosaurus indicate that it may have been up to 40 percent larger than Kronosaurus, with estimates of overall length of 55–66 feet/17–20 m in length and a weight of 50 tons.

See Appendix B for references used for collating this information.

Genesis 1:21 declares: "And God created great whales, and every living creature that moveth, which the waters brought forth abundantly." The Hebrew word translated "whales" is actually the word for "dragon." In the first chapter of the first book of the Bible, God is describing His creation of the great dragons (sea-dwelling dinosaur-like animals).

There is a mention of a flying serpent in Scripture:

. . . and fiery flying serpent (Isa. 30:6).

This could be a reference to one of the dinosaur-type creatures that flew, such as the *Pteranodon* or *Rhamphorhynchus.*[39]

Pteranodon

Pteranodon

The Pteranodon pictured here is a flying reptile, not a dinosaur, and has been classified as belonging to the Class: Reptilia; Infraclass: Archosauromorpha; Superorder: Archosauria; Order: Pterosauria; Suborder: Pterodactylidea; Family: Ornithocheiridae or Pteranodontidae (depending on reference); Genus: Pteranodon.

Pteranodon

Pteranodons [te-RAN-oh-don] and all the other flying reptiles that we find in the fossil record were created on day five of creation as we read in Genesis 1:20–23: "And God said, Let the waters bring forth abundantly the moving creature that hath life, and fowl that may fly above the earth in the open firmament of heaven. And God created great whales, and every living creature that moveth, which the waters brought forth abundantly, after their kind, and every winged fowl after his kind: and God saw that it was good. And God blessed them, saying, Be fruitful, and multiply, and fill the waters in the seas, and let fowl multiply in the earth. And the evening and the morning were the fifth day."

Pteranodon, meaning "winged and toothless" or "toothless flier," was among the largest of the flying reptiles, with nearly 30-foot wingspans in some species and estimated weights of up to 40 pounds. It is easily recognized by the huge bony crest on the back of the skull. One specimen had a skull and crest that measured 5 feet 9 inches in length.

Pteranodon was rediscovered in 1870 when O.C. Marsh and Colonel William F. Cody ("Buffalo Bill") traveled from Yale College (as it was known then) to the chalk beds of western Kansas. Marsh found the fossil remains of large marine reptiles (*plesiosaurs* and *mosasaurs*) and the broken finger bones of a *pterosaur*. He recognized the finger bones as being similar to those found in Europe, but he was puzzled by the fact that they indicated a much larger *pterosaur* (a wingspan of 23 feet) than those found in Europe. Within two years, both Marsh and Cope (Marsh's rival) had recovered enough *pterosaur* remains to allow them to name the specimen. As these two famous paleontologists had already been bitterly feuding with each other for some years, they each chose a different name. In 1872, Marsh named his specimen *Pterodactylus* in reference to the European type and Cope named his specimen

Ornithochirus, meaning "bird arm." After more material was collected by S.W. Williston for Marsh, and studied, he decided to rename his specimen *Pteranodon,* meaning "winged and toothless" because of the huge wingspan and long, pointed toothless beak (most *pterosaurs* have teeth).

Originally, scientists thought that the huge crest of the *Pteranodon* was somehow used in the aerodynamics of flight. More recently, however, the consensus is that it acted as a counterbalance for the long beak. Evolutionists theorize that *Pteranodon* would glide on wind currents over open water since all of their remains have been found in sedimentary layers (evolutionists believe these to be evidence of ancient oceans and seas). Of course, creationists believe that these sedimentary deposits resulted from the flood of Noah's day. Evolutionists also theorize that this creature would use its long beak to pluck fish out of water. Without the crest to counterbalance the head and beak, it is thought that the head would be snapped off when the beak was dipped into the water. Did these creatures eat fish before the Fall? Not if fish are regarded as having a nephesh, i.e., being alive in the biblical sense.

There were many different types and sizes of flying reptiles that have been found in the fossil record. Some of these match eyewitness descriptions of people such as the Greek historian Herodotus and the prophet Isaiah. In Isaiah 30:6 we read, "The burden of the beasts of the south: into the land of trouble and anguish, from whence [come] the young and old lion, the viper, the fiery flying serpent, they will carry their riches upon the shoulders of young asses, and their treasures upon the bunches of camels, to a people that shall not profit [them]."

> Though Isaiah was speaking figuratively, he used living animals that were well known to the people as his symbols.
>
> See Appendix B for references used for collating this information.

Summary:

People down through the ages have been familiar with dragons. The descriptions of these animals fit with what we know about dinosaurs. The Bible even mentions such creatures (even the ones that lived in the sea and flew in the air) more than many other animals. This is tremendous historical evidence that such creatures have lived beside people.

Large Carnosaur Skeleton

WHAT DID DINOSAURS EAT, AND HOW DID THEY BEHAVE?

*M*ovies like *Jurassic Park* and *The Lost World* portray most dinosaurs as aggressive meat eaters. But just the presence of sharp teeth in an animal does NOT tell you how it behaved, or what food it ate — only what kind of teeth it had (for ripping food). By studying fossil dinosaur dung (coprolite),[40] scientists have even been able to determine the diet of some of the dinosaurs.

Bible Reading: Genesis 1:29–31.

Originally, before sin, ALL animals including the dinosaurs were vegetarian. Genesis 1:30 states: "And to every beast of the earth, and to every fowl of the air, and to every thing that creepeth upon the earth, wherein there is life, I have given every green herb for meat: and it was so."

This means that even *T. rex*, before sin entered the world, ate only plants. Some people object to this clear, biblical teaching by pointing to the six-inch-long teeth that a large *T. rex* had, insisting they must have been used for

attacking animals. However, just because an animal has large, sharp teeth, doesn't mean it was (or is) a meat-eater; it just means it has big, sharp teeth.[41]

There are many animals today that have sharp teeth but are basically vegetarian, including the Chinese panda. Evolutionists often make the comment that the panda evolved as a meat-eater, so it could get sharp teeth, but which it now uses to mainly eat bamboo.[42] On the other hand, creationists could argue that the panda's teeth are beautifully designed to chew bamboo.

Flying foxes (fruit bats) have long, sharp teeth like those of vicious meat-eating animals, yet their diet consists solely of fruit.[43]

Skull of a fruit bat

Bears have the same sort of teeth structure as a big cat (e.g., lion), but some bears are vegetarian, and others are mainly vegetarian.[44]

As has already been discussed, there were no flesh-eaters before sin. The world's animals (including dinosaurs) and the first two people lived in perfect harmony. In fact, the Bible's description of the world before sin was called "very good" (Gen. 1:31).

Some people cannot accept this perfect, harmonious description of the world because of the food chain they observe today. However, one cannot look at our sin-cursed world, and the resultant death and struggle, and use this to reject a literal reading of Genesis. The fact is, everything has changed because of sin. Instead, one must look at the world through the Bible's "eyes."

For example, Paul describes the present creation as "groaning" (Rom. 8:22).

Most people (including most Christians) tend to observe the world as it is today, with all its death and suffering, and then take that observation TO the Bible and interpret it in that light. In reality, we are sinful, fallible human beings, observing a sin-cursed world (Rom. 8:22), and thus look at the Bible through the world's "eyes"!

A true Christian world view commences with REVELATION,[45] not human opinion! (For example, take a pair of eyeglasses and pretend they represent the Bible and its time-line of history. Put on the glasses and look at the world — you are looking at the world through the Bible's "eyes" — not looking at the world through the world's "eyes"!)[46]

WHAT ABOUT CHARACTERISTICS OF ANIMALS TODAY THAT SEEM TO BE SUITED FOR HUNTING AND KILLING?

As creation scientist Dr. Henry Morris states: "Whether such structures as fangs and claws were part of their original equipment, or were recessive features which only became dominant due to selection processes later, or were mutational features following the Curse, or exactly what, must await further research."[47]

After sin entered the world, everything changed. Maybe some creatures started eating other animals at this stage. By the time of Noah's day, God described what had happened in this way: "And God looked upon the earth, and, behold, it was corrupt; for all flesh had corrupted his way upon the earth" (Gen. 6:12).

For we know that the whole creation groaneth and travaileth in pain together until now.

Romans 8:22

Also, in Genesis 9:2 (after the flood), God changed the behavior of animals. We read, "And the fear of you and the dread of you shall be upon every beast of the earth, and upon every fowl of the air, upon all that moveth upon the earth, and upon all the fishes of the sea; into your hand are they delivered."

WHY DO WE FIND DINOSAUR FOSSILS?

*T*he formation of fossils is basically a catastrophic event. When an animal dies, it usually decays until there is nothing left. To form a fossil, however, unique conditions are required to preserve the animal and replace it with minerals, etc.

Evolutionists used to claim that the fossil record was laid down slowly as animals died and were covered by sediment. But in more recent times they have admitted that the fossil record necessarily involves catastrophic processes.[48] To form the billions of fossils we see worldwide (in layers sometimes miles thick), the organisms, by and large, must have been buried quickly. Evolutionists now are basically saying that the fossil record formed quickly, but over millions of years!

According to the biblical record, the earth after the Fall became full of wickedness. God determined He would send a worldwide (global) flood "to destroy all flesh wherein is the breath of life, from under heaven" (Gen. 6:17). He commanded a man named Noah to build a very large boat into which he would take his family and representatives of all land-dwelling, air-breathing animals (that God himself would choose and send to Noah).

The Bible tells us clearly that when the time for the flood came, God sent two of every kind of animal (and seven of some[49]) to Noah to take up residence aboard the ark (Gen. 7:2–3). Since the Bible is clear that there were at least two of every kind of land animal, this must have included two of every KIND of dinosaur.

Many people think that most dinosaurs were large creatures, and thus would never have fit into the ark. But the truth of the matter is that the average size of a dinosaur (based on the skeletons all over the earth) is about the size of a sheep.[50] Many dinosaurs were quite small. For instance, *Struthiomimus* was only the size of an ostrich, and *Compsognathus* was no bigger than a rooster! Only a few dinosaurs grew to extremely large sizes (e.g., *Diplodocus, Apatosaurus, Allosaurus*), but even they were not as big as the largest animal in the world today, the blue whale. (Some reptiles and some amphibians continue to grow the entire time they are alive; the large dinosaurs may have been very old dinosaurs.)

Dinosaurs laid eggs, and the biggest fossil dinosaur egg ever found was about the size of a foot-

ball.[51] Even the large dinosaurs were very small when they first hatched. It is realistic to assume that God would have sent young adults on the ark, not fully grown creatures. Since the animals that came off the boat were to be responsible for re-populating the earth, it was probably young adults that were on board, which would be in the prime of their reproductive life.

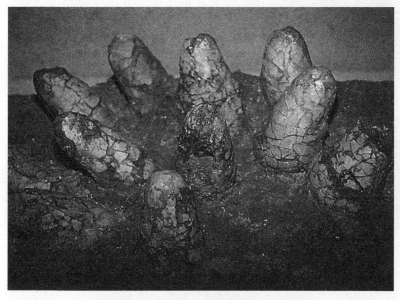

Protoceratops andresnsi eggs

This baby dinosaur hatching from the egg is a Stegosaurus, which means "roof lizard." It belongs to the Class: Reptilia; Infraclass: Archosauromorpha; Superorder: Archosauria; Order: Ornithischia (bird-hipped dinosaurs); Suborder: Stegosauria or Thyrephora (depending upon the reference); Family: Stegosauridae

Baby Stegosaurus

STEGOSAURUS

Stegosaurus [Steg-oh-SORE-us] was created on day six of the creation week, over 6,000 years ago, along with the rest of the land animals and man, as we read in Genesis 1:24–31, "And God said, Let the earth bring forth the living creatures after his kind, cattle, and creeping thing, and beast of the earth after his kind: and it was so. And God made the beast of the earth after his kind, and cattle after their kind, and every thing that creepeth upon the earth after his kind: and God saw that it was good. And God said, Let us make man in our image, after our likeness: and let them have dominion over the fish of the sea, and over the fowl of the air, and over the cattle, and over all the earth, and over every creeping thing that creepeth upon the earth. . . . And God saw every thing that he had made, and, behold, it was very good. And the evening and the morning were the sixth day."

There were a number of different species of *Stegosaurus*, and they varied in size and type of plates and spikes along the back and tail. The most popular and well-known was *Stegosaurus stenops*, which had the traditionally drawn double row of large arrowhead-shaped plates on the back running from the base of the head to the tail (which was armed with only two pair of spikes). Since the plates were not attached to the skeleton, how they were positioned is unclear. The tail spikes in some *Stegosaurs* reached 4 feet in length and are thought to have been able to be wielded like a spiked club, probably as a defensive weapon. The average *Stegosaur* was about 20 feet long, with some reaching 30 feet. They weighed approximately two U.S. tons. The skull was about 16 inches long, was very narrow and contained small cheek teeth and a toothless beak at the front.

The hind legs were usually twice as long as the front legs, giving the *Stegosaurus* a sloping appearance of always walking downhill. They had tall spines that projected upward from the vertebrae of the hip and base of the tail. These probably served as attachment points for the large and powerful muscles of the back and hindquarters, and could even have allowed for the *Stegosaurus* to have lifted its front feet off the ground, allowing it to feed off the lower branches of trees. A number of *Stegosaur* specimens have been found with bony ossicles, about the size of buttons, covering the throat area and elsewhere on the body (such as over the thighs and tail), which could have given the animal some protection like a natural chain mail.

Another characteristic of *Stegosaurs* was the "second brain" or sacral plexus. There was a large cavity (up to 20 times larger than the actual brain) within the hip that is believed to have contained a large collection of nerve tissue. The purpose of this "second brain" is unclear. Theories have ranged from a brain controlling the rear half of the animal (especially since its real brain only weighed between 2.5 to 2.8 ounces and was no larger than a walnut, and according to O.C. Marsh had the smallest brain-to-body ratio of any land vertebrate) to a center for neural control of muscle coordination (as in the ostrich). Some have even suggested that the cavity in the hip housed a gland that may have produced glycogen, which would have been a useful source of energy for the massive muscles of the hindquarters. The truth is that there was simply a cavity in the hip and we haven't a clue what was in it or what it did!

The plates along its back provide another area of speculation for which no function is known. Some scientists believe that the plates may have been covered with a tough horn-like covering, similar to the horns on cattle, as a means of protection. Others think that they were covered with a layer of blood-rich skin and that by aligning them with the sun or against the sun, could have been used for heat regulation. Frankly, all we know is that *Stegosaurs* had huge bony plates on their backs!

Stegosaurs were rediscovered in 1876 in Quarry 1 in Fremont County, Colorado, by Marsh and was described by him in 1877 (the *Stegosaurus* happens to be the state fossil of Colorado). The largest concentration of *Stegosaurs* was located in 1879 at what came to be known as Quarry 13 in Albany County, Wyoming. This quarry was worked till 1887 by William H. Reed under the supervision of Marsh.

Stegosaurus specimens can be seen on display at the American Museum of Natural History in New York City; Carnegie Museum of Natural History in Pittsburgh, Pennsylvania; Denver Museum of Natural History in Denver, Colorado; Dinosaur National Monument in Jensen, Utah; Peabody Museum of Natural History in New Haven, Connecticut; Smithsonian Institution (National Museum of Natural History) in Washington, DC; University of Michigan Exhibit Museum in Ann Arbor, Michigan; and the Utah Museum of Natural History (University of Utah) in Salt Lake City, Utah.

As you look at this baby *Stegosaurus* hatching from its egg, think of how easy it would have been for Noah to have taken a number of dinosaurs (that normally grow very large) on the ark. We know that all dinosaurs start out small. It is only after many years of growth that they attain gigantic sizes. Quite possibly, a "teenage" dinosaur, just coming into its age of reproduction, was much smaller (e.g., the size of a small pony) than an older giant *Stegosaurus*. People don't doubt that Noah took bulls and horses on board the ark, so if they start their thinking with the Bible, why should they doubt that he also took dinosaurs?

See Appendix B for references used for collating this information.

Some might argue that there would have been too many dinosaurs to fit on the ark. After all, they say, there are over 600 different names of dinosaurs.[52] In Genesis 6:20, the Bible states that representative "kinds" of land animals boarded the ark. But what is a "kind"? Biblical creationists have pointed out that there can be many "species" within a "kind"[53] — e.g., there are many types of cats in the world, but all cat "species" may have come from only a few "kinds" of cats originally.[54]

The cat varieties today have developed by natural and artificial selection acting on the original variability in the information (genes) of the original cats, resulting in differing combinations of information, and thus, speciation. Therefore, only a few "cat" pairs may have been needed on Noah's ark.

This "speciation" is NOT "evolution," since it is based strictly on the created information already present, and is thus limited. Evolution from amoeba to man, however, requires new information to arise, and by natural processes. Put another way; one involves thinning of gene pools (natural selection/speciation), the other an expansion (evolution). Thus, for dinosaurs (or any other creature) to evolve, there would have to be a mechanism to produce information from disorder by chance (this has NEVER been observed to happen), and continually add in new information so new types could evolve.

But true science has only observed that it takes information to produce information — information NEVER arises by chance.[55] Thus, the evolution (in the Darwinian sense) of dinosaurs is impossible.

Protoceratops skull

NUMBER OF 'KINDS' OF DINOSAURS

M any of the dinosaur names are given to just a few pieces of bone, or a skeleton that looks similar to another one but is a different size, or perhaps in a different country.[56] After carefully investigating the different dinosaur finds, it seems there were probably about 50 distinct groups or "kinds" of dinosaurs that needed to be represented on the ark.

In addition, it must be remembered that Noah's ark was extremely large. In their classic book *The Genesis Flood*, Drs. Henry Morris and John Whitcomb calculated the approximate size of the ark and the number of animals needed to represent all the kinds. Their calculations suggest that fewer than 75,000 individual animals (more than enough for all the "kinds") could have fit on only one floor of the ark, since their average size would have been no bigger than a sheep (actually, the average size of a land animal is much less than this).[57] The ark was more than large enough to carry representatives of every kind of air-breathing, land-dwelling animal.[58]

The land animals (including dinosaurs) that didn't go on the ark, of course, drowned. Many of their bodies were preserved in the layers formed by flood, thus the billions of fossils. Presumably, many of the dinosaur fossils that have been found were buried at this time, around 4,500 years ago. Also, after the flood, there would have been considerable catastrophism, including such things as the Ice Age,[59] resulting in additional (post-flood) formation of fossils.

The twisted and contorted shapes of these animals preserved in the rocks, the massive numbers of them in fossil graveyards (and their wide distribution), and the presence of whole skeletons which show convincing evidence of being buried rapidly, all testify to massive flooding.[60]

IS THERE ANY EVIDENCE OF DINOSAURS LIVING AFTER THE FLOOD?

At the end of the flood, Noah, his family, and the animals came out of the ark (Gen. 8:15–17). The dinosaur kinds thus began a new life in a new world. Two by two, the dinosaurs, along with all the other animals, came out to breed and re-populate the earth. They would have left the landing place of the ark and moved over the earth's surface. The descendants of these dinosaurs gave rise to the dragon legends.

But the world into which they emerged was different from the one they knew before Noah's flood. It had been ravaged by water violence. It would be a much more difficult world in which to survive.

Again, dinosaurs were living on the earth at the same time as people. Not that long after the flood a man called Job heard God describe a great creature that Job was obviously familiar with. God was showing Job how great He was as Creator, in causing him to observe the largest land animal He had made:

> "Behold now behemoth, which I made with thee; he eateth grass as an ox. Lo now, his strength is in his loins, and his force is in the navel of his

belly. He moveth his tail like a cedar: the sinews of his stones are wrapped together. His bones are as strong pieces of brass; his bones are like bars of iron. He is the chief of the ways of God: he that made him can make his sword to approach unto him" (Job 40:15–19).The phrase "chief of the ways of God" means this was the largest animal God had made. So what kind of animal was "behemoth"?

In the notes of many Bible commentaries, "behemoth" is said to be an elephant or a hippopotamus.[61] Besides the fact that these were NOT the largest land animals God made (as far as we know, some of the dinosaurs were the largest land animals that ever existed), this description doesn't make sense, since behemoth is said to have had a tail like a cedar (verse 17).

Now if there's one thing an elephant's tiny tail (or a hippo's tiny tail, which looks like a flap of skin!) is unlike, it is a cedar tree! The elephant and the hippo are thus quickly eliminated as possibilities for this beast. There are Hebrew words for elephant or hippopotamus, but the Bible did not use these terms. Because the translators did not know what this beast was, they transliterated the Hebrew, and thus came the word "behemoth."

After reading this passage of Job very carefully, one is hard put to find any LIVING creature that comes close to fitting this description. The closest animal could be something like *Brachiosaurus*, one of the dinosaurs.

At the time the King James Bible was translated, dinosaurs had not yet been "rediscovered," and the word "dinosaur" had not been invented. Sadly, some of the modern translations (and paraphrases) of the Bible change the word translated "behemoth" in the KJV to "hippopotamus" or "elephant."[62] In fact, a number of animals in some translations are probably incorrect, because the translators were influenced by evolutionary teaching, and wouldn't consider the names of animals they thought died out millions of years ago (before man) in the translation.

Isn't it sad that evolutionary indoctrination so permeates even the thinking of Christians, that translators would go against the obvious in reading Job 40, and put in the name of an animal contradicted by the description?

Foot of a Saurolophus

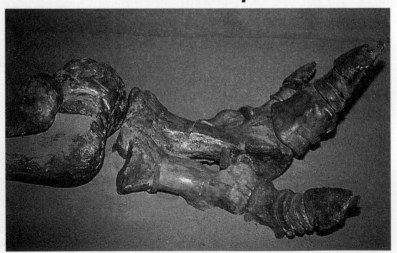

Behemoth

The Behemoth portrayed here is a Brachiosaurus [brak-EE-oh-SORE-us] which means "Arm Reptile." Class: Reptilia; Infraclass: Archosauromorpha; Superorder: Archosauria; Order: Saurischia (Lizard-hipped dinosaur); Suborder: Sauropodomorpha; Infraorder: Sauropoda; Family: Brachiosauridae.

BEHEMOTH

The *Behemoth* [beh-HE-moth] is described in Job 40:15–24: "Behold now behemoth, which I made with thee; he eateth grass as an ox. Lo now, his strength is in his loins, and his force is in the navel of his belly. He moveth his tail like a cedar: the sinews of his stones are wrapped together. His bones are as strong pieces of brass; his bones are like bars of iron. He is the chief of the ways of God: he that made him can make his sword to approach unto him. Surely the mountains bring forth food, where all the beasts of the field play. He lieth under the shady trees, in the covert of the reed, and ferns. The shady trees cover him with their shadow; the willows of the brook compass him about. Behold he drinketh up a river, and hasteth not: he trusteth that he can draw up Jordan into his mouth. He taketh it with his eye; his nose pierceth through snares."

Brachiosaurus measures in at an enormous 75 feet in length and 41 feet in height, weighing about 89 U.S. tons, three times heavier than an *Apatosaurus* and as much as 12 modern adult African bull elephants! Its shoulders were 21 feet off the ground and its humerus (upper arm bone) was 7 feet long.

Once thought to be the largest land animal ever, *Brachiosaurus* may now be dwarfed by two new sauropods. *Supersaurus* and *Ultrasaurus*, having 8-foot-long shoulder blades and 5-feet-long vertebrae, may have exceeded 100 feet in total length.

At least one pair of sauropods went on Noah's ark as we read in Genesis 7:13–15, "In the selfsame day entered Noah, and Shem, and Ham, and Japheth, the sons of Noah, and Noah's wife, and the three wives of his sons with them, into the ark; they, and every beast after his kind, and all the cattle after their kind, and every creeping thing that creepeth upon the earth after his kind, and every fowl after his kind, and every bird of every sort. And they went in unto Noah into the ark, two and two of all flesh, wherein is the breath of life." It is very possible that they were young ones and still small enough to easily fit on board.

Brachiosaurus was created on day six with the other land animals, beasts, and creeping things. It was rediscovered in 1900 in the Grand River Valley of western Colorado. It was collected by a team from the Field Museum in Chicago and later named by Elmer S. Riggs in 1903. The specimen consisted of various parts of the vertebral column, the pelvis, ribs, shoulder girdle, humerus, and femur. "Judging by the way the remains were preserved on site, it appeared that the original carcass of the animals probably settled into the sediment of a lake or river system in this area, but was disturbed somewhat later, perhaps by flood water, so that various parts of it were washed away as the carcass disintegrated, and so lost to us forever" (Norman, p. 89).

The humerus was 80 inches long and the femur was only 79.5 inches. In all other sauropods except the *Brachiosaurus*, the femur is always longer than the humerus. *Brachiosaurus* differs from all other sauropods in that the front legs are longer than the hind legs, which makes the back slope backwards, much like that of a giraffe. In all other sauropods, the hind legs are longer than the front, giving them more of an arched shape to their body. Because of the unusual difference in size, the humerus was first identified as the femur. It wasn't until they were preparing the specimen in the museum that they realized it was the humerus. Unlike other sauropods, such as the *Diplodocus* whose hindlegs supported most of the weight (78 percent compared with only 22 percent for the front legs), *Brachiosaurus* had a more even weight distribution between front and back limbs (52 percent for the hind legs compared to 48 percent for the front). The head was dome-shaped with a wide snout. The teeth were peg-like and pointed. Like all other sauropods, the two nasal openings are in the top of the skull, above the eyes. This trait led many scientists to believe that most of the sauropods, including *Brachiosaurus*, were amphibious. However, that idea has been re-evaluated in the past 20 years and they are now considered to be terrestrial.

Another interesting feature of the *Brachiosaurus* is the vertebrae. They were hollowed-out in many areas, leaving only enough bone in the strategic places to give the necessary support and strength. Thus, the vertebrae were lightweight, yet strong enough to withstand the tremendous stress they were under. According to one author: "The secret of supporting such a massive body lay in the construction of *Brachiosaurus'* backbone. Great chunks of bone were hollowed out from the sides of each vertebra, to leave a structure, anchor-shaped in cross section, made of thin sheets and struts of bone. The resulting skeleton was a master-piece of engineering — a lightweight framework, made of immensely strong, yet flexible, vertebrae, each angled and articulated to provide maximum strength along the lines of stress." (Dixon p. 128–129)

The structure of the long neck (which is longer than its tail) shows that it did not have a great deal of flexibility. This is characterized by the long cervical ribs and undivided neural spines which seem to indicate that the neck was ventrally braced. The greatest amount of flexibility would have come from the occipital area and the shoulder area.

The large size of the *Brachiosaurus* would also have some consequences on its blood pressure and body temperature. Being able to raise its head nearly 25 feet above its heart would have meant that its blood pressure would have to have been much higher than many other dinosaurs and most likely may have possessed some special features similar to those found in giraffes. However, this is speculation since we do not have the soft tissue to see what special features God designed in them for the control of blood pressure.

Another feature of the large size would have been a fairly constant body temperature. The larger the animal, the slower the body heats up and cools down. With the great size of the *Brachiosaurus*, even with a reptilian-like (cold blooded) metabolism, it probably would have maintained a fairly constant temperature.

In 1907 an engineering geologist by the name of W.B. Sattler was searching the colony of German East Africa (known today as Tanzania) when he discovered a number of large fossil bones at Tendaguru. He immediately contacted his company, which in turn brought in Professor Eberhard Fraas from Stuttgart, Germany, to examine the finds. He collected a few specimens and returned to Germany.

In 1908, Dr. W. Branca, then director of the Berlin Museum of Natural History, sent Drs. Werner Janesch and Edwin Hennig to the area where they worked until 1912, carefully excavating a number of fossils and returning them to the Berlin Museum. Among the specimens they collected at Tendaguru were *Kentrosaurus, Elaphrosaurus, Dicraeosaurus*, and *Brachiosaurus*. The *Brachiosaurus* was assembled and is on display at the Natural History Museum in Berlin. This *Brachiosaurus* stands 39 feet tall and is 74 feet long. To fossilize such a large animal would certainly take a catastrophic event (Noah's flood?) to quickly cover and preserve such massive remains.

See Appendix B for references used for collating this information.

REASONS FOR
EXTINCTION

Genesis states that after the flood, God told Noah that from then on the animals would fear him, and man could eat their flesh (Gen. 9:1–7). There were yet more changes because of sin! Even for man, the world had become a harsher place. In order for him to survive, the once easily obtained plant protein would now have to be supplemented by animal sources. Man went into competition with the animals to survive.

Both animals and man would find their survival ability tested to the utmost. It is a fact of history deducible from the fossil record, from the written history of man, and from experience over recent centuries, that not all species of life on this planet have survived that competition.

While we know that vast numbers of marine species became extinct at the time of Noah's flood, we need to remember that many plants and air-breathing, land-dwelling animals have become extinct only since the flood, either due to man's action, competition with other species, or because of the harsher post-flood environment. Many groups are still becoming extinct. Dinosaurs are certainly numbered among the creatures that seem to no longer exist.

Why then do people get so intrigued about the disappearance of dinosaurs, and have very little interest in the extinction, for example, of the fern *Archaeopteris*?[63]

If it were not for their size and "appeal" as monsters, dinosaurs would have excited no more than passing interest. However, because of mankind's almost "science fiction" fascination with the unusual, dinosaurs have become famous throughout the world. People are fascinated with the question: *What really did happen to them?*

Evolutionists have capitalized on this dinosaur fascination, and have inundated the world with evolutionary propaganda centered around dinosaurs. This has resulted in even Christians being permeated by evolutionary philosophy. As a result, they tend to single out the dinosaurs as something mysterious. However, there is NOTHING mysterious about them, if we build our thinking on the Bible.

Think about it. If you were to go to a zoo and ask why it has an endangered species program, you would probably get an answer something like this:

"Endangered species programs! Why, it's obvious! We've lost lots of animals from this earth. Animals are becoming extinct all the time. We need to act to save the animals. Look at this long list of animals that are gone forever."

If you then asked, "Why are animals becoming extinct?" you might get an answer like this: "Why, it's obvious! People killing them, lack of food, man destroying the environment, diseases, genetic problems, catastrophes like floods — there are lots of reasons."

Then if you said, "Well, can you tell me what happened to the dinosaurs?" the answer would probably be, "We don't know! Scientists have suggested dozens of possible reasons — but we don't know."

Maybe one of the reasons dinosaurs are extinct is because we didn't start our endangered species programs early enough! The point is — the same reasons that cause extinction today — all as a result of man's sin, the Curse, the effects of the flood (a judgment), etc. — are the same reasons that caused the dinosaurs to become extinct — if they really are all extinct.

Triceratops

The Triceratops belongs to the Class: Reptilia; Infraclass: Archosauromorpha; Superorder: Archosauria; Order: Ornithischia; Suborder: Ceratopia or Marginocephalia (depending upon reference); Family: Ceratopsidae; Genus: Triceratops.

TRICERATOPS

Triceratops [Try-SER-ah-tops], like all the land animals, was created on day six of creation and lived with Adam and Eve in the Garden of Eden. This dinosaur, which looks like a cross between a bull and a rhinoceros, was also on Noah's ark (Gen. 7:13–15).

There have been as many as 16 different species listed, but many scientists now feel that there may be only one species, *horridus*, and maybe a second, as yet unnamed, species. The differences between them have been largely due to the differences of sex and age of the individuals.

Triceratops is one of the most easily recognized and more popular of the dinosaurs. It possessed massive horns — two above the eyes and one on the snout. *Triceratops* means "three-horned face" from the Greek *tri* = three + *keratos* = horn + *ops* = face. The horns on some of the *Triceratops* have reached lengths of over three feet. It is thought that the bony cores to the horn had a hardened sheath of material over them similar to cattle, especially since a 1–2 cm thick, carbonaceous powdery layer was found surrounding the horn of a young *Triceratops*.

The large plate that extends up from the back of the head and covering the neck is called the "frill." Frills have been found that vary greatly in size and shape, from small frills with smooth edges to large frills with knobby bones, called epoccipital bones, on the edge. Some *Triceratops* have skulls with frills that measure 6 feet 6 inches long and 7 feet across. Because of the massiveness of the skulls, they were prime candidates for fossilization. They have sharp, parrot-like beaks in the front of the mouth, formed from the rostral and predentary bones, which would have been hardened with a horn-like covering, forming a sharp cutting surface. They had leaf-shaped teeth in the back, and apparently very powerful jaw muscles. In fact, some scientists believe that part of the function of the frill was for the attachment of the powerful jaw muscles. Others believe it to be a protective shield for the head and neck, and others believe that they also served as heat regulators.

Triceratops have been found that were 30 feet in length and estimated to weigh as much as 11 U.S. tons. For years the front legs were shown as being splayed out wide; however, more recent studies have indicated that they were more in a straight down formation. This shape of the front legs would have allowed for the *Triceratops* to move much quicker than earlier thought, but fossilized footprints found thus far do not show a very fast-moving animal. Yet tests done on the leg bones of *Triceratops* give "strength indicators" of 12–21 units, indicating the ability to gallop. (As a comparison, the African buffalo tests at 21–27 units and is quite mobile.) The phalangeal formula is 2-3-4-5-0. The claws were broad, flat, and hoof-like.

Triceratops was discovered in the 1880s in Montana by O.C. Marsh. The first fossil remains found consisted of horn cores. Thinking that they belonged to a mammal, Marsh named them *Bison alticornis.* When more of the remains were found and studied, he renamed it *Triceratops* in 1889. Their fossil skulls were very abundant; it was reported that Barnum Brown had found over 500 *Triceratops* skulls. Brown once commented, "During seven years' work, 1902–1909, in Hell Creek Beds of

Montana, I identified no less than 500 fragmentary skulls and innumerable bones referable to this genus" (Norell, p. 172). A number of the skulls found had broken and damaged horns and frills that showed evidence of healing, which has given support to the idea that they used their horns for defense or for sparring with each other during mating season, or both.

Finding over 500 skulls of one dinosaur in just seven years is a tremendous testimony to the severity of the effects that sin has had on this world and the judgment that it brought.

In Genesis, chapters 6 and 7, we read:

And God saw that the wickedness of man was great in the earth, and that every imagination of the thoughts of his heart was only evil continually. And it repented the LORD that he had made man on the earth, and it grieved him at his heart. And the LORD said, I will destroy man whom I have created from the face of the earth; both man, and beast, and the creeping thing, and the fowls of the air; for it repenteth me that I have made them. . . .

And it came to pass after seven days, that the waters of the flood were upon the earth. In the six hundredth year of Noah's life, in the second month, the same day were all the fountains of the great deep broken up, and the windows of heaven were opened. And the rain was upon the earth forty days and forty nights.

And the flood was forty days upon the earth; and the waters increased, and bare up the ark, and it was lifted up above the earth. And the waters prevailed, and were increased greatly upon the earth; and the ark went upon the face of the waters. And the waters prevailed exceedingly upon the earth; and all the high hills, that were under the whole heaven, were covered. Fifteen cubits upward did the waters prevail; and the mountains were covered.

And all flesh died that moved upon the earth, both of fowl, and of cattle, and of beast, and of every creeping thing that creepeth upon the earth, and every man. All in whose nostrils was the breath of life, of all that was in the dry land, died. And every living substance was destroyed which was upon the face of the ground, both man, and cattle, and the creeping things, and the fowl of the heaven; and they were destroyed from the earth: and Noah only remained alive, and they that were with him in the ark.

And the waters prevailed upon the earth an hundred and fifty days."

When we look at the fossils of these dinosaurs and other animals destroyed by the judgment on man's sin, it should remind us that we, too, are under that same type of judgment. It is only through the saving blood of Jesus Christ that we can obtain salvation.

Fossils of *Triceratops* have been found in Montana, Colorado, Wyoming, and South Dakota in the United States, and in Alberta and Saskatchewan in Canada. They were the most abundant group of large herbivores from the Late Cretaceous layers found in western North America.

It is thought that they followed a lifestyle similar to the buffalo, traveling in herds and following migration routes. Many also believe that they would take up a protective position around their young when danger threatened. Others believe that although they may have been one of the most abundant dinosaurs in North America, they may have had only loosely organized populations without necessarily moving in herds. It should be noted here that all of these behavioral aspects are speculations based upon assumptions that cannot be verified, because no one recorded these behaviors.

Triceratops skeletons are on display at the American Museum of Natural History in New York (this display is actually made from the parts of seven different skeletons; the lower jaw from one, neck vertebrae from a second, skull from a third, and the remainder of the skeleton was compiled from four other skeletons); Buffalo Museum of Science in Buffalo, New York; National Museum of Natural Sciences in Ottawa, Canada; Smithsonian Institution (National Museum of Natural History) in Washington DC; Birmingham Museum in Birmingham, United Kingdom; National Museum of Natural History (Institut de Paléontologie) in Paris, France; Natural History Museum (British Museum) in London, United Kingdom; Senckenberg Nature Museum in Frankfurt, Germany; Royal Scottish Museum in Edinburgh, Scotland; and Hunterian Museum in Glasgow, Scotland.

See Appendix B references used for collating this information.

ARE DINOSAURS EXTINCT?

It is hard to say categorically that any animal is extinct, since scientists can't possibly go everywhere on this planet and simultaneously declare an animal to have disappeared entirely. Geologists, the traditional declarers of extinction, have been severely embarrassed several times when, after having declared animals to be extinct,

they have discovered them alive and well in environments the scientists merely hadn't searched. Explorers
recently found elephants in Nepal that have the characteristics of mammoths![64]

Scientists in Australia found some living trees that they
had thought became extinct at the time of the dinosaurs.
One scientist said "It was like finding a live dinosaur."[65]

It needs to be emphasized that it is neither possible
nor feasible to have one person at every point on the
earth's surface looking in every direction all at one time,
just to be 100 percent sure that
there are no dinosaurs,
and that, therefore, di-
nosaurs truly are ex-
tinct.

There have been
present-day reported
sightings of what might be
dinosaur-type animals.[66]

In *Science Digest*, 1981,
and in *Science Frontiers*, no.
3367, explorers and natives in Af-
rica have reported sightings of dinosaur-like creatures.
These have usually been confined to out-of-the-way
places such as lakes in the middle of the Congo jungles.
But descriptions given certainly fit those of dinosaurs.

Cave paintings done by Indians in America seem to
clearly depict a dinosaur.[68] Since scientists accept the
mammoth drawings done by Indians, why not the dinosaur-
like drawings? However, evolutionary indoctrination that
man didn't live at the same time as dinosaurs precludes
evolutionary scientists even considering these drawings as
dinosaurs that lived at the same time as the Indians.

It could even be true that the Loch Ness monster (if Nessie really exists) is a variety of *Plesiosaur*, which still survives today. And it certainly would be no embarrassment to a creationist if someone discovered a living *Tyrannosaurus rex* in a jungle. It wouldn't even be surprising if it happened to be a plant-eater! However, this would be a tremendous embarrassment to an evolutionist.

When scientists do find animals or plants they thought were extinct millions of years ago, they call them "living fossils." There are now hundreds of documented "living fossils" that have become an embarrassment for evolutionists.[69]

And no, we couldn't clone a dinosaur even if we had dinosaur DNA as the fictional movie *Jurassic Park* portrayed — not unless there already was a living female dinosaur. Scientists have found that to clone an animal, they must have an egg of a living female, as there is machinery in the cytoplasm of the egg that is necessary for the creature to develop.[70]

Actually, evolutionists don't really think dinosaurs are extinct anyway! At the entrance to the bird exhibit at the Cincinnati Zoo in Ohio, one reads the following sign:

"Dinosaurs went extinct millions of years ago
— or did they?
No — birds are essentially modern short-tailed
feathered dinosaurs."

In the mid-1960s, Dr. John Ostrom from Yale University in the USA, began to popularize the idea that dinosaurs evolved into birds.[71]

Not all evolutionists agree with this assessment though. "It's just a fantasy of theirs," says Alan Feduccia, an ornithologist at the University of North Carolina at Chapel Hill, and a leading critic of the paleontologists. "They so much want to see living dinosaurs that now they think they can study them vicariously at the backyard bird feeder."[72]

There have been many recent attempts to indoctrinate the public in believing that modern birds are really dinosaurs. *Time* magazine in 1993 featured a front-page cover of a "birdosaur" with feathers (a supposed transitional form between dinosaurs and birds) based on a fossil find that had NO feathers, but in the same month *Science News* had an article suggesting this animal was only a "mole."[73]

In 1996 newspapers reported on a find in China[74] of a reptile fossil that supposedly had feathers. Some of the media reports claimed that, if it was confirmed, it was "irrefutable evidence that today's birds evolved from dinosaurs."[75] One scientist stated publicly, "You can't come to any conclusion other than that they're feathers."[76] However, in 1997 the Academy of Natural Sciences in Philadelphia sent what they called "the dream team" (four leading scientists) to investigate this find.[77] And the result of their investigation? They were NOT feathers. Concerning one of the scientists, the media reported "He said he saw 'hair-like' structures — not hairs — that could have supported a frill, or crest, like those on iguanas."[78]

No sooner had this report appeared than another media story claimed that 20 fragments of bones of a reptile found in South America showed that dinosaurs were related to birds![79]

One of the reasons there has been so much debate in scientific circles about whether dinosaurs were warm-blooded or cold-blooded centers around the bird/dinosaur debate. Because birds are warm-blooded, evolutionists who believe dinosaurs evolved into birds would like to see dinosaurs as warm-blooded to support their particular theory.

A media report quoting Dr. Larry Martin of the University of Kansas stated that "recent research has shown the microscopic structure of dinosaur bones was 'characteristic of cold-blooded animals.' " He continued "So we're back to cold-blooded dinosaurs."[80]

Sadly, the secular media has become so blatant in its anti-Christian stand and evolutionary propaganda that they are bold enough to make such incredible statements as, "Parrots and hummingbirds are also dinosaurs."[81]

Several new reports have fueled the bird/dinosaur debate among evolutionists. One report concerns the research on the embryonic origins of the fingers of birds and dinosaurs showing they could NOT be evolved from dinosaurs![82] A second report was based on a study of the photographs of the so-called feathered dinosaurs from China which revealed that the dinosaur had a distinctive reptilian lung and diaphragm which is very different from the avian lung.[83] A third report showed that the frayed edges that some thought to be feathers on the China fossil are

similar to the collagen fibers found immediately beneath the skin of sea snakes and therefore offer another viable explanation instead of them being feathers.[84]

There is NO evidence dinosaurs evolved into birds. Dinosaurs have always been dinosaurs!

WHY DOES IT MATTER?

Although the subject of dinosaurs is fascinating, some who read this book may say, "Why are you making this topic such a big deal? Surely there are many more important issues to deal with in today's world, such as abortion, homosexual behavior, euthanasia, suicide, lawlessness, pornography, and so on. Shouldn't dealing with these social issues that plague our culture be the priority? In fact, we should be telling people about the gospel of Jesus Christ, rather than worrying about side issues like dinosaurs!"

Actually the evolutionist teachings on dinosaurs that are presented through the education system and media DO have a great bearing on why many won't listen to the gospel, and why social issues like those mentioned above are so prevalent in our culture today.

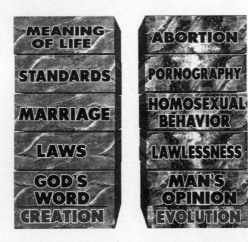

One of the purposes of this book is to show that the evolutionist teachings on dinosaurs cannot be defended, but if one accepts God's Word, beginning with Genesis, as true and authoritative, then one CAN explain dinosaurs and make sense of the evidence we observe in the world around us. In doing this, we are also showing that Genesis is absolutely trustworthy and logically defensible, and is what it claims to be — the true account of the history of the universe and mankind. What one believes concerning the Book of Genesis will ultimately determine what one believes about the rest of the Bible. This in turn will affect how a person views him or herself and fellow human beings, their future, and what life is all about.

THE IMPLICATIONS

If one accepts the atheistic evolutionist teachings on dinosaurs, then God's Word (the Bible) is not authoritative, and all things can be explained by natural processes — there is no God! Thus, there is no absolute authority. The following are just a few of the implications of accepting this position:

1. WHY IS THERE RIGHT AND WRONG?

In the New Testament in Matthew 19:16–17, a man came to Jesus and said to Him, "Good Master, what good thing shall I do, that I may have eternal life?" Jesus replied, "Why callest thou me good? there is none good but one, that is, God."

How do you decide if something is right or wrong or good or bad? God, the only one who is good, created us and therefore owns us. Thus, we are obligated to Him and we must obey Him. He has a right to set the rules. He knows everything there is to know about everything (has absolute knowledge), and therefore we must obey.

That is why we have absolutes, why there are standards, and why there is right and wrong.

When people are taught that there is no God, that all things can be explained by natural processes, and that death and struggle are the order of the day, then this logically will affect one's view of morality. If there is no God, then there is no basis for right and wrong. In the Old Testament Book of Judges, we read that when the people had no king to tell them what to do, then they all did what was right in their own eyes.

When there is no absolute authority, then a person can do whatever is convenient to them — if they can get away with it.

The more people reject God and believe an evolutionary view of origins, the more they could logically say, "There is no God. Why should I obey authority? No one owns me — I own myself. Why should there be rules against what is called aberrant sexual behavior? Why should there be rules against abortion? After all, evolution tells us we are all animals. So killing babies by abortion is the same as chopping off the head of a fish or chicken. Why shouldn't I do whatever I want with sex? I can decide my own rules for life."

Thus, as people logically apply the teaching of atheistic evolution in their own lives, one could expect to see an increase in the acceptance of lawlessness, abortion, and pornography in the culture. This is exactly what is happening!

2. WHAT IS MARRIAGE ALL ABOUT?

*W*hen Jesus was asked concerning marriage and divorce in Matthew 19: 4–5, we read, "And he answered and said unto them, Have ye not read, that he which made them at the beginning made them male and female, And said, For this cause shall a man leave father and mother, and shall cleave to his wife: and they twain shall be one flesh?"

Jesus quoted directly from Genesis, chapters 1 and 2. What He was saying was this: "Don't you understand — the reason for marriage is that there is a historical basis." If we didn't have this historical basis, there wouldn't be such an institution as marriage. Thus, if a person is not a Christian (or does not believe in a literal Genesis) and yet believes in the marriage doctrine of one man for one woman for life — then they are inconsistent in their thinking, as the only basis that marriage must be one man for one woman for life is based upon the absolute authority of God's Word in Genesis. Now one could say that marriage was convenient to you — but how could you tell your son, for instance, that he couldn't marry Bill! There is no justification for this outside of accepting a literal Genesis.

As we read Genesis, we are told how God took dust and made the first man. From the man's side He then made the first woman. They were one flesh. Adam's first recorded words were, "This is now bone of my bones, and flesh of my flesh." That is why, when a couple is married, the couple becomes one — it has a historical basis. If Genesis is not true, there can be no oneness in marriage.

Also, the married couple are to cleave unto each other just as if they had no parents. Just like Adam and Eve who had no parents. We know it is to be a heterosexual relationship ONLY. Why? Because God made Adam and Eve, not two men or two women, but one man and one woman. That is the only basis for marriage and that is also why we know that homosexual behavior is evil, a perverse and unnatural deviancy.

However, the more people reject the Book of Genesis (and the rest of the Bible) as God's authoritative Word, then the more we would expect to see people rejecting God's foundation for marriage. There is no doubt that the acceptance of homosexual behavior is on the rise in Western culture. This goes hand in hand with the increasing acceptance of evolutionary teaching and its consequence of the undermining of the authority of the Bible.

FOUNDATIONS UNDER ATTACK

*I*n reality, the evolutionary teaching on dinosaurs is an attack on the foundations of Christianity. Psalm 11:3

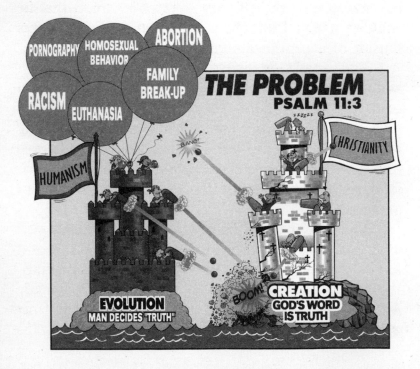

states, "If the foundations be destroyed, what can the righteous do?" If you destroy the foundations of anything, the structure will collapse. If a person wanted to destroy any building, the best way would be to destroy the foundation. Likewise, if someone wanted to destroy Christianity, then they would need to destroy the foundations which are established in the Book of Genesis.

The biblical doctrine of origins, as contained in the Book of Genesis, is foundational to all other doctrines of Scripture. Refute or undermine in any way the biblical doctrine of origins, and the rest of the Bible is undermined. Every single biblical doctrine of theology, directly or indirectly, ultimately has its basis in the Book of Genesis. Therefore, if one does not have a believing understanding of that book (not just believing it is true, but believing and understanding what it says), then one cannot hope to attain full understanding of what Christianity is all about. People fool themselves if they think they understand what Christianity is all about but don't understand the Book of Genesis.

The reason for this is that the meaning of anything is tied up with its origins. If you want to understand the meaning of anything, you must understand its origins — its basis. Genesis is the only book that provides an account of the origin of all the basic entities of life and the universe such as the origin of life, of man, of government, of marriage, of culture, of nations, of death, of sin, and of clothes.

The meaning of all these things is dependent on their origin. In the same way, the meaning and purpose of the Christian gospel depends on the origin of the problem for which the Savior's death was and is the solution.

MILLIONS OF YEARS AND THE GOSPEL

*T*he teaching that dinosaurs lived and died millions of years before man is in actuality a direct attack on the foundations of the gospel. The fossil record in which we find dinosaurs consists of billions of dead creatures. In fact, it is a record of death, disease, suffering, cruelty, and brutality. It is a very ugly record.

Evolutionary scientists claim the fossil layers over the earth's surface date back hundreds of millions of years. As soon as one allows for the millions of years for the fossil layers — then one has accepted death, bloodshed, disease, and suffering before Adam's sin.

The Bible makes it clear that death, bloodshed, disease, and suffering are a consequence of sin. In Genesis 1:29–30 we read that Adam and Eve and the animals were told only to eat plants (This is reading Genesis and taking it at face value, as literal history, as Jesus did in Matthew 19:4–6.) In fact, there is a theological distinction made between animals and plants. Human beings and animals are described in Genesis 1 as having a "nephesh," or life principle. (This is true of the land animals as well as the birds and sea creatures: Genesis 1:20–24.) Plants do not have this "nephesh" — they are not "alive" in the same sense animals are. They were given for food. (Man was told he could eat meat for the first time in Genesis 9:3 — this also makes it obvious that the statements in Genesis 1:29–30 were meant to inform us that man and the animals were vegetarian to start with. Also in Genesis 9:2 we're told of a change God made in the way animals react to man.)

God warned Adam in Genesis 2:17 that if he ate of the "tree of the knowledge of good and evil," he would "die." The Hebrew word for "die" actually means, "dying, you will die." In other words, it would be a process of dying.

After Adam disobeyed God, then the Lord clothed Adam and Eve with "coats of skins" (Genesis 3:21). To do this He must have killed and shed the blood of at least one animal. The reason for this can be summed up by Hebrews 9:22:

> *And almost all things are by the law purged with blood; and without shedding of blood is no remission.*

God required the shedding of blood for the remission of sins. What happened in the garden was a picture of what was to come in Jesus Christ, who shed His blood on the cross to be the Lamb of God, "which taketh away the sin of the world" (John 1:29).

Now if there was the shedding of blood before sin, as there would have been if the garden was sitting on a fossil record of dead things millions of years old, then this would destroy the foundation of the atonement. This also fits with the fact that Paul states in Romans 8 that the whole of creation "groaneth" because of the effects of the fall of Adam.

Jesus Christ suffered physical death and shed His blood because death was the penalty for sin. Paul discusses this in detail in Romans 5 and 1 Corinthians 15.

Revelation, chapters 21 and 22, make it clear that there will be a "new heaven and a new earth" one day in the future where there will be "no more death" and "no more curse" — just like it was before sin changed everything. Obviously, if there are going to be animals as part of the new earth, they will not be dying or eating each other or the redeemed people!

Thus, the teaching of millions of years of death, disease, and suffering before Adam sinned is a direct attack on the foundations of the message of the Cross.

MISSIONARY LIZARDS!

Dinosaurs are probably used more than anything to brainwash people — including young children — in these evolutionary ideas of chance random processes producing life, and millions of years of death and suffering.

Sadly, I have found over and over that people, particularly students at schools and colleges and universities, say that because of evolution, the Bible must be wrong.

Because of the huge number of evolutionary books on dinosaurs, and movies like *Jurassic Park* and *The Lost World*, the secular world and even the Church have been indoctrinated to believe evolutionary ideas. For many, this has become one of the biggest stumbling blocks to believing the Bible — which is usually presented as an outdated anti-scientific book that has no relevance for modern man. Thus, the message of salvation is being scoffed at more and more.

Also, because most churches have allowed evolutionary ideas, and not taught the foundational importance of the Book of Genesis, nor the truth about dinosaur history based upon the Bible, people aren't sure they can trust the Bible. When confronted by skeptics, they don't know what to say. There is a deadness in their life. They can't defend the Bible, so the people they are talking to assume they don't have to take the Bible seriously.

Christians are often confused, and don't know what to say to their children. So, sadly, the next generation grows up accepting evolution and oftentimes

DINOSAURS...

Missionary Lizards!

rejecting the claims of the Bible and thus Christianity.

The truth is that dinosaurs are easily explained and understood when the Bible is used as the foundation for thinking. Not only can answers be given about when they lived, how they died, etc., they can be used as MISSIONARY LIZARDS. The Bible and its account of the history of the universe can be shown to be trustworthy — right from the beginning (from Genesis).

Christians can show the world that the evolutionist story about dinosaurs cannot be defended, but the biblical account presents a logically defensible account that makes sense of the evidence.

At the same time, one can talk about the origin of death, the entrance of sin, the ark of salvation in Noah's time, and the ark of salvation for us — the Lord Jesus Christ, and the wonderful message of eternal life with the Lord in heaven.

We can use dinosaurs as a witnessing tool to present the gospel of Jesus Christ, so that people can be led to say with John:

> *These things have I written unto you that*
> *believe on the name of the Son of God;*
> *that ye may know that ye have eternal*
> *life, and that ye may believe on the name*
> *of the Son of God*
> (1 John 5:13).

Telling people the true history of the world from the Bible and presenting the solution to the world's problems — the wonderful message of the Christian gospel — is what this book is all about.

What Is a Christian?

*B*ecoming a Christian is more important than anything else in life. From then on, whatever happens to you in this world, you will know that you are forever safe and secure in the Lord Jesus Christ, and even when death comes, you shall be with Him forever.

How can I become a Christian?

*F*irst, we need to understand the true history of humanity that has been revealed to us in the Bible (Genesis 1–3). The infinite God created the heavens and the earth in six days, just a few thousand years ago. On the sixth day, the Lord God also created the first humans, Adam and Eve, from which every generation in this world has descended. Adam was the head of the entire human race. Adam and Eve were created perfect, without sin. They had a perfect relationship with their Creator. The tragedy is that our original parents did not remain in their righteousness and purity as the Lord made them.

They were enticed to rebel against their Creator by a created being called Satan. He is not, however, all powerful, does not have all knowledge, and is not present everywhere. Originally, Satan was not created evil, but he also rebelled against his Creator. Satan was working hard in the Garden of Eden (where God had placed Adam and Eve) for the whole purpose of overturning the order of creation. Satan now is an evil personal being, and together with the other evil beings, their purpose is to stand against the truth of God and oppose the Lord's people.

It was not long before Adam and Eve committed sin (disobedience) against the Lord. Their responsibility before God was their own! Adam's sin brought death, and death has proceeded to every single person — every descendant of this first man.

Because of Adam's sin, death (in a spiritual sense) was immediate, for he was severed in his relationship with the Lord. We need to understand that this is not just coming from our perspective, but that a Holy God could no longer have a relationship with people who are in sin. The Bible is clear, "The soul that sinneth, it shall die" (Ezek. 18:20).

Physical death came as a result of sin. "Wherefore, as by one man sin entered into the world, and death by sin; and so death passed upon all men, for that all have sinned" (Rom. 5:12). Sin is simply rebellion against the Lord. Such rebellion has been in every person's life. The Bible tells us, "The imagination of man's heart is evil from his youth" (Gen. 8:21). The Book of Jeremiah declares, "The heart is deceitful above all things, and desperately wicked: who can know it?" (Jer. 17:9).

After Adam and Eve's rebellion, God promised a resolution to this severed relationship in the sending of the Savior, the Lord Jesus Christ. "And I will put enmity between thee and the woman, and between thy seed and her seed; it shall bruise thy head, and thou shalt bruise his heel" (Gen. 3:15).

Because a man (Adam) brought sin and thus death into the world, a man would be needed to pay the penalty for sin. The penalty, however, could only be paid by a perfect man — but all descendants of Adam would be sinners. God's solution was to send His Son (God who became flesh, the Lord Jesus Christ), born of a virgin, to be a perfect man (without sin), and yet a descendant of Adam.

Genesis 3:15 is actually looking forward to the coming of Christ (who was to be the new head, taking Adam's place) into this world and the ultimate defeat of Satan. Every person is responsible for him/herself before the Lord. Every person knows that the living God exists, but many either reject or neglect this absolute truth. "Because that which may be known of God is manifest in them; for God hath shewed it unto them." (Rom. 1:19). The reality is that people who trust in Christ will be with Him forever, but people who reject or neglect Christ will be forsaken for eternity.

The wonderful thing is that God sent Christ into this world for one main purpose: to bring repentant sinners into a true relationship with the Lord. The Lord Jesus Christ came to bring salvation. His birth into this world was very special. He was born of a virgin by the power of the Holy Spirit; no human male was involved (Matt. 1:18–21). From His birth to His death, He was without sin and yet at the same time, He was all of man, (i.e., a true human, and yet all of God). This is why He was one with us, because He was all of man, and yet remaining perfect; the only one who could, on our behalf, die for our sin, to remove the death that is the result of sin, to defeat Satan.

On the cross, His blood was shed, for He was the true sacrifice which God had already purposed (Acts 2:23). The cross on which He died was a curse, and He was forsaken by the Father, that you and I shall never be forsaken. He died and was buried, but life is in God, and the Lord Jesus Christ rose from the dead triumphantly and is alive today and forevermore. He is the Sovereign Lord, and He will come again to receive His people to himself.

WHAT DO I NEED TO DO?

First, I Need to Repent!

Repentance is essential. It really means "a change of mind." For me to be saved by Christ, I must turn from my self-centeredness, and from any desire that takes priority over the Lord Jesus Christ. Repentance means a complete turning around from where I was as a person (focused on myself), to submit and yield my life to the only living God. I must admit that I am a sinner, in rebellion against the Lord God.

In Philippians 3:8, the apostle Paul makes a statement that needs to apply to each of us as individuals: "Yea doubtless, and I count all things but loss for the excellency of the knowledge of Christ Jesus my Lord: for whom I have suffered the loss of all things, and do count them but dung [rubbish], that I may win Christ."

Repentance is absolutely necessary. That's why we can understand when the Lord Jesus came into this world, He spoke these words, "The time is fulfilled, and the kingdom of God is at hand: repent ye, and believe the gospel" (Mark 1:15). Repentance is necessary for every person to become a Christian. Some people say that so long as I confess my sin, I'll be okay. But dear friend, this is not sufficient.

The Book of Proverbs tells us, "He that covereth his sins shall not prosper, but whoso confesseth and forsaketh them shall have mercy" (Prov. 28:13). Repentance is a complete turning from my former life, and a full desire to live in the righteousness of the Lord. Righteousness means "justice, straight, right." In other words, it simply means living the same life that the Lord Jesus lived. He was without sin. He was pure, holy, just, righteous. The life of the Lord Jesus is that quality of life that each of us needs to imitate in every respect. The Spirit of God was within Him, and He constantly displayed the reality of His life: love, joy, peace, patience, kindness, goodness, faithfulness, gentleness, and self-control (Gal. 5:22–23;NIV). He was never conceited, neither did He provoke or envy other people. He always lived the truth of God, and spoke the truth.

Although we are people who are committed to our Savior, the Lord Jesus Christ, we nevertheless will still sin regularly. When we know we are truly trusting Christ, forgiveness is real. The Bible tells us, "If we say that we have no sin, we deceive ourselves, and the truth is not in us. If we confess our sins, he is faithful and just to forgive us our sins, and to cleanse us from all unrighteousness" (1 John 1:8–9).

Second, I Need to Put My Faith in Christ

Faith really means to trust, and to believe in the Lord Jesus Christ. I need to trust in Christ and rely on Him alone. Faith is like an instrument the Lord provides by which we can believe in Christ. I am not brought into salvation because of my own doing. No! It is because our loving Lord has poured His grace and mercy upon me. Grace is something I freely receive from the Lord — it is God showing His favor on us without our meriting it. Although I deserve nothing from the Lord, and I have no ability to boast, the gift of salvation comes to me through faith. Faith is that instrument or that channel that the Lord gives me by which I can trust and believe in the Lord Jesus Christ. The Bible tells us, "For by grace are ye saved through faith; and that not of yourselves: it is the gift of God: not of works, lest any man should boast" (Eph. 2:8–9).

The Book of Romans points out that I am "justified freely by His grace" (Rom. 3:24). This simply means that through faith I am declared righteous in the sight of God. Many years ago, Augustus Toplady wrote a great hymn, "Rock of Ages." One of the lines he wrote is: "Nothing in my hand I bring, simply to the Cross I cling." The only merit that can get me to heaven is the merit of Jesus Christ alone. It is absolutely essential for each of us to focus on the Lord Jesus Christ and trust and believe in Him alone.

Third, I Need to Pray

Prayer is very important. Prayer means that a true believer can speak to our Lord at any time. Satan will try his hardest to stop you from praying. Prayer is really the breath of your soul. If your breath/prayer is taken away, you have nothing. Cultivating a habit of prayer is essential. All of us need to regularly turn our eyes to the Lord Jesus Christ in prayer.

There are many prayers in the Bible. Often it is very helpful to follow the examples of prayers, such as Matthew 6:9–13 and Ephesians 3:14–21. There are many things I will need to thank the Lord for. Daily I should thank Him for my salvation, my life, and my family. I can always ask the Lord for strength, help, guidance, and wisdom. It is also necessary to pray for others who are in difficulty, or who need to know the Lord Jesus Christ.

Why not pray now, repent of your sin, receive Christ, and accept what He has done for you in His death and resurrection?

• • • • •

After receiving Christ, you will find that Bible reading is essential. By regularly studying the Bible, which is God's written revelation to us, you will grow in your salvation. It is important to find a church where the Bible is constantly read and preached, and where you can enjoy fellowship with the Lord's people. The Bible says, "Wherewithal shall a young man cleanse his way? By taking heed thereto according to thy word" (Ps. 119:9).

It is a privilege to love and serve the Lord. Service does not just mean going to church. Service for the Lord means the desire to live a holy life for Christ, encouraging and building up one another. Also, to engage in the sharing of the gospel of Christ with other people is a wonderful experience.

How Can I Be Sure That I'm a Christian?

We read these words in 1 John 5:13, "These things have I written unto you that believe on the name of the Son of God; that ye may know that ye have eternal life, and that ye may believe on the name of the Son of God."

Jesus said, "I am the way, the truth, and the life: no man cometh unto the Father, but by me" (John 14:6). My desire must be to humble myself before the Lord in true repentance, with a sincere trust and belief in the Lord Jesus Christ alone. A Christian will display the evidence of living the life that Jesus lived, and even though I sin, there will be a sorrow in my life because of sin, and as I confess this before the Lord, forgiveness has already belonged to me. The Lord says, "For I will forgive their wickedness and will remember their sins no more" (Heb. 8:12; 1 John 2:12).

I must certainly show that my life is different to the people of the world. As Christians, "Let us not love in word, neither in tongue; but in deed and in truth" (1 John 3:18). We know that we belong to the truth when our lives are resting in the presence of Christ (1 John 3:19). Obedience to the Lord through the Bible is the quality of a Christian. As a Christian, I must persevere in faith, with true Christian living until the end, and be eternally saved.

My focus must be on the Lord Jesus Christ, with a desire for holiness and a true love for my neighbor. This certainly points to the genuineness of being a Christian, and reassures us of our security in Christ. The Bible says, "For I am persuaded, that neither death nor life, nor angels, nor principalities, nor powers, nor things present, nor things to come, nor height, nor depth, nor any other creature, shall be able to separate us from the love of God, which is in Christ Jesus our Lord" (Rom. 8:38–39).

If you trusted the Lord Jesus Christ after reading this publication, or would like to know more about becoming a Christian, (or about understanding the Bible better), write us. Addresses are listed at the end of this book.

The Consequence of Compromise

Now that you've finished this book, I trust you can see that when one believes and understands the events of history as given in the Bible, and the basic Christian doctrines, then it really is easy to give answers when asked about dinosaurs.

But what happens when Christians don't believe the Bible's history or understand the doctrines of Christianity that are based in Genesis? For instance, what about people who are Theistic Evolutionists,[85] Progressive Creationists,[86] or Gap Theorists[87]? All these ideas accept death, bloodshed, disease, and suffering before sin, and to one degree or another add aspects of what evolutionists teach into their thinking. Also, many who hold these positions do not accept Noah's flood as global, but only a local event.

There are also many Christians who say they don't know what to believe about Genesis, chapters 1–12.

Well, if someone holds one of the positions above, they should consider the following illustration about a conversation between a father and son:

"Hey, Dad, I had a lesson on dinosaurs at school today. How should I, as a Christian, understand these creatures?"

"Well, Son — I don't really know. Didn't they live millions of years ago?"

"That's what they say, Dad. But how does all this fit with the Bible?"

"Well, Son, I'm sure we can accept the scientists' view and not affect our belief in the Bible, can't we?"

"I don't know, Dad. I mean, if what the scientists say is true, then does that mean the Bible is not accurate in Genesis when it talks about creation, the Flood, and the ark?"

"Son, look. The Bible tells us why God created — not how. We have to leave that up to the scientists."

"Okay, Dad. But what parts of the Bible can I trust? Did we all really come from Adam? How can there be a God of love as I learn at church, when we see all this suffering in the world?

"How do you explain all the 'races' of people on the earth? How should I understand the Grand Canyon? Did coal really form over millions of years? There seem to be too many animals to fit on Noah's ark — is this story just a fairy tale?

"Why is marriage supposed to be only between a man and a woman? Why, Dad? If I'm a sinner as the Bible says, what does this mean? Where did sin come from? Is the Bible just a book about salvation? How do I know that's even true? I'm confused, Dad!"

But the Christian Dad who believes God's Word and understands that all his thinking is built ON the Bible (STARTING with Genesis) DOES have ANSWERS — LOTS of answers! And not just answers about dinosaurs — but answers to the basic questions about life and the universe.

APPENDIX A
DINOSAUR FACTS AND THEORIES

The following collection of facts and theories on dinosaurs provide detailed and very up-to-date documentation for the information contained in the text of this book. We have not only provided the reference for you, but also a summary of what was stated in the particular publication/research paper. This

Trilobite

provides students, teachers, and other researchers with a very valuable collection of material for research projects, assignments, etc., on the topic of dinosaurs.

1 John R. Horner and Don Lessem, *The Complete T. rex* (New York: Simon & Schuster, 1993,) p. 18. "Dinosaurs may be among the most long-lived and successful animals ever to walk the earth. But they didn't come along until 235 million years ago."

Don Lessem and Donald F. Glut, *The Dinosaur Society's Dinosaur Encyclopedia* (New York: Random House, Inc., 1993), p. ix. "The oldest known dinosaur fossils are found in rocks about 230 million years old, and dinosaur footprints occur in rocks even older than that."

Mark A. Norell, Eugene S. Gaffney, and Lowell Dingus, *Discovering Dinosaurs in the American Museum of Natural History* (New York: Nevraumont Publ. Co., Inc., 1995), p. 17. "What is the earliest-known dinosaur? The best-documented candidates are from the Late Triassic

Ischigualasto Formation of Argentina. Fossils found in these beds include the theropods *Herrerasaurus* and *Eoraptor*, as well as the ornithischian *Pisanosaurus*. The Ischigualasto beds contain a volcanic ash that has recently yielded a radiometric date of 228 million years ago."

2 Alan Feduccia, *The Origin and Evolution of Birds* (New Haven, CT: Yale University Press, 1996), p. 28. "As Professor Othniel Charles Marsh of Yale University wrote in 1877: 'The classes of Birds and Reptiles, as now living, are separated by a gulf so profound that a few years since it was cited by opponents of evolution as the most important break in the animal series, and one which that doctrine could not bridge over. Since Huxley has clearly shown, this gap has been virtually filled by the discovery of bird-like Reptiles and reptilian Birds. *Compsognathus* and *Archaeopteryx* of the Old World . . . are the stepping stones by which the evolutionist of today leads the doubting brother across the shallow remnant of the gulf, once thought impassable.' "

Duane T. Gish, *Evolution: the Fossils Still Say No!* (El Cajon, CA: Institute for Creation Research, 1995), p. 130. "John H. Ostrom has been most instrumental in advancing the theory that birds evolved from a small coelurosaurian dinosaur similar to *Compsognathus*.

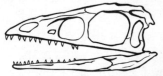

Compsognathus

Today the notion that birds evolved from dinosaurs is so widely accepted that some have suggested that birds, rather than being placed in the Class Aves, should be relegated to a position within the Dinosauria. In fact, it is being commonly maintained that dinosaurs still survive today in the form of birds, their feathered offspring." Norell et.al., *Discovering Dinosaurs in the American Museum of Natural History*, p. 2. "Dinosaurs belong to a group called *Archosauria. Archosaurs* are divided into two groups, the *Crurotarsi* (crocodiles and their relatives) and the *Ornithodira*, a group com-

posed predominantly of *pterosaurs* and dino- saurs. The living *Archosauria* are the 21 extant crocodiles and alliga- tors, along with the more than ten thousand species of living thero- pod dinosaurs (birds)." Norell et.al., *Discovering Dinosaurs in the American Museum of Natural History*, p. 11. "Accord- ing to one story, one Christmas Day Huxley was carving a turkey for his annual feast. As he dis- sected the drumstick he was struck by the unmistakable simi-

Archaeopteryx

larity between his Christmas dinner and the fossils of the theropod *Megalosaurus* back in his office. From that day on Huxley proclaimed (to use his own stiff Victorian words), ' . . . surely there is nothing very wild or illegiti- mate in the hypothesis that the phylum of the class Aves has its roots in the dinosaurian reptiles.' "

Giovanni Pinna, translated by Jay Hyams, *The Illustrated Encyclopedia of Fossils* (New York: Facts on File, Inc., 1990), p. 219–220. "Because birds possess many of the traits of their reptilian predecessors they have been called 'glorified reptiles.' But they are in fact different, not only because of their feathers, but also due to a more evolved physiology. They are warm-blooded animals, which allows them far greater activity than their predecessors, who may, in fact, have been warm-blooded dinosaurs, according to current evidence. Some authorities even believe birds to be the last surviving lineage of dinosaurs, that they should not be placed in a separate class."

3 Russell D. Humphreys, *Starlight and Time* (Green Forest, AR: Master Books, 1996), p. 83, Appendix C — "Progress Toward a Young-Earth Relativistic Cosmology" as presented to the Third International Conference on Creationism, 1994. "As measured by clocks on earth, the age of the universe today could be as small as the face-value biblical age of about 6,000 years."

Henry M. Morris, *The Genesis Record* (Grand Rapids, MI: Baker Book House, 1976), p. 42–46. This section of Morris' book discusses "The Date of Creation" and concludes with this statement: "Consequently, the account of earth history as recorded in Genesis fixes the creation of the universe at several thousand, rather than several billion, years ago. The exact date may be as long ago as 10,000 B.C., or as recently as 4000 B.C., with the probabilities (from biblical considerations, at least) favoring the lower end of this spectrum."

Archbishop James Ussher, *The Annals of the World* (London: Printed by E. Tyler for F. Crook and G. Bedell, 1658). Ussher used biblical data, chronologies, and genealogies to calculate the date of creation at 4004 B.C.

4 Genesis 1:24–31. "And God said, Let the earth bring forth the living creature after his kind, cattle, and creeping thing, and beast of the earth after his kind: and it was so. And God made the beast of the earth after his kind, and cattle after their kind, and every thing that creepeth upon the earth after his kind: and God saw that it was good. . . .

And God saw every thing that he had made, and, behold, it was very good. And the evening and the morning were the sixth day."

5 Genesis 1:20–23. "And God said, Let the waters bring forth abundantly the moving creatures that hath life, and fowl that may fly above the earth in the open firmament of heaven. And God created great whales, and every living creature that moveth, which the waters bring forth abundantly, after their kinds, and every winged fowl after his kind: and God saw that it was good. And God blessed them, saying, Be fruitful, and multiply, and fill the waters in the seas, and let fowl multiply in the earth. And the evening and the morning were the fifth day." We are clearly told that those creatures of air and waters were created on day five. This would have included the marine reptiles such as the *Plesiosaur*, *Kronosaurus*, and *Leviathan* along with the flying reptiles such as the *Pteranodon*, *Pterodactyl*, and *Rhamphorhynchus*.

6 Romans 5:12–14. "Wherefore, as by one man sin entered into the world, and death by sin; and so death passed upon all men, for that all have sinned. . . . Nevertheless death reigned from Adam to Moses, even over them that had not sinned after the similitude of Adam's transgression, who is the figure of him that was to come."

1 Corinthians 15:21–22. "For since by man came death, by man came also the resurrection of the dead. For as in Adam all die, even so in Christ shall all be made alive."

Ken Ham, *The Lie: Evolution* (Green Forest, AR: Master Books, 1987), p. 71–72. "As a result of that rebellion in Eden, a number of things happened. First, man was estranged from God. That separation is called spiritual death. On its own, the final effect of this would have been living forever in our sinful bodies, eternally separated from God. Imagine living with Hitler and Stalin forever! Imagine living in an incorrigible, sinful state for eternity. But something else happened. Romans 5:12

tells us that as a result of man's actions came sin, and as a result of sin came death; but not just spiritual death, as some theologians claim. To confirm this, one needs only read 1 Corinthians 15:20 where Paul talks about the physical death of the first Adam and the physical death of Christ, the last Adam. Or read Genesis 3, where God expelled Adam and Eve from the Garden so that they would not eat of the Tree of Life and live forever. Physical death as well as spiritual death resulted from their sin."

James Stambaugh, "Creation, Suffering and the Problem of Evil," *Creation ex nihilo Technical Journal*, Vol. 10(3), 1996, p. 391–404. Stambaugh discusses the theological implications of the origin of evil and suffering and how it, and death, resulted from the sin of Adam, ruining God's perfect creation.

7 Michael Benton, *Dinosaurs: An A-Z Guide* (New York: Derrydale Books, 1988), p. 10. "At the beginning of the Triassic period, 245 million years ago, there were no dinosaurs. The Earth was ruled by several primitive groups of reptiles. These all died out about 20 million years later, and the dinosaurs arose to importance. During the age of the dinosaurs, 200 million years ago, the continents were all joined together to form one land mass."

David Lambert and the Diagram Group. *The Dinosaur Data Book* (New York: Avon Books, 1990), p. 10–35. "THE AGE OF DINOSAURS — After an overview of dinosaurs, these pages trace the origins of backboned

CREATIONWISE

animals leading to the rise of reptiles and the Mesozoic Era or Age of Dinosaurs. We see how dinosaurs themselves evolved and how they differed from all other reptiles. A glance at their close kin *pterosaurs* and birds leads to a grand family tree of dinosaurs and their relations. Then come brief accounts of the lands, climates, plants, and animals that shared the world with dinosaurs through the three periods of Mesozoic time. The chapter ends with a selection of solutions to prehistory's greatest riddle: why dinosaurs died out 65 million years ago." This entire chapter traces the supposed history of nearly 170 million years of earth history, based entirely on the fossil and geologic records of the present.

Norell et.al., *Discovering Dinosaurs in the American Museum of Natural History*, p. 62–69. "Why did non-avian dinosaurs become extinct? . . . Nobody knows for sure. Many ideas have been proposed, but scientific tests to decide which idea is the most reasonable are difficult to conduct. For example, one hypothesis is that non-avian dinosaurs became extinct because they got hay fever from flowering plants, which arose and became common during the Cretaceous. We have no way to determine if dinosaurs got hay fever. As far as we know, living dinosaurs do not, and fossils tell us nothing about this idea." The next seven pages then proceed to cover some of the major theories of dinosaur extinction, all of which are based on evidences from the fossil and geologic records, of which exist in the present, not in the past.

Virgil L. Sharpton and Peter D. Ward, editors, *Global Catastrophes in Earth History; An Interdisciplinary Conference on Impacts, Volcanism, and Mass Mortality,* The Geological Society of America, Special Paper 247, 1990, p. ix-x. "One of the liveliest topics of scientific debate throughout the 1980s has been the issue of catastrophic events and mass mortality, particularly with regard to the K/T boundary. . . . Literally hundreds of papers have addressed related topics ranging from mechanics of impact cratering, to studies of trace-element geochemistry, to atmospheric modeling, to understanding the detailed patterns of faunal and floral extinction at the K/T and other stratigraphic boundaries. In addition, many new arenas have been opened: shocked minerals have been detected in conjunction with the geochemical anomaly at the K/T boundary, periodicities have been reported in both the marine extinction record and the terrestrial impact record, enhanced levels of iridium have been measured in volcanic aerosols. . . . this volume contains the peer-reviewed papers that grew from this conference. Of the 75 manuscripts submitted for publication, 58 were finally accepted. . . . It is clear from these proceedings that much progress has been made since the first Snowbird Conference in many diverse fields, and although the K/T boundary continues to dominate research, this volume makes equally clear that many new themes and lines of evidence continue to emerge." The rest of this book is a 600+ page treatise on the various theories of extinction and catastrophes in earth history, all based upon the evidence we have in the present.

8 Psalm 78:5. "For he established a testimony in Jacob, and appointed a law in Israel, which he commanded our fathers, that they should make them known to their children."

  2 Timothy 3:16. "All scripture is given by inspiration of God, and is profitable for doctrine, for reproof, for correction, for instruction in righteousness."

  2 Peter 1:21. "For the prophecy came not in old time by the will of man: but holy men of God spake as they were moved by the Holy Ghost."

9 Titus 1:2, "In hope of eternal life, which God, that cannot lie, promised before the world began."

10 Paul Hoffman, Paul, "Fowl Play," *Discover*, May 1992, p. 4. "The truth is that even if you find a totally complete

CREATIONWISE

dinosaur skeleton, you can't just string it together. To do that, you'd have to know exactly how its muscles, cartilage, and ligaments were arranged — and those are gone forever. Any reconstruction is a hypothesis. . . . As theoretical as this kind of work is, arranging these kinds of fossils is the relatively easy part of paleontology. What you don't see in museum displays are the scores of headless, legless, ribless, smashed, crushed, and half-digested fossils that paleontologists depend on for much of their knowledge of extinct life. Many researchers find themselves sifting through piles of bones of animals that were washed down ancient rivers — mishmashes of many kinds of small creatures — trying to decide which piece goes with which."

11 Dougal Dixon, Barry Cox, R.J.G. Savage, and Brian Gardiner, *The MacMillan Illustrated Encyclopedia of Dinosaurs and Prehistoric Animals* (New York: Macmillan Publishing Co., 1988), p. 92. "Various systems of classification were proposed for them [dinosaurs], but it was not until 1887 that another English anatomist, Harry Seeley, recognized that there were 2 distinct types of hip girdle or pelvis. In some, dinosaurs, the pelvis was of a normal reptilian build, so Seeley called this group the *Saurischia*, or 'lizard-hipped' dinosaurs. In others, the pelvis resembled that of modern birds, and so he called them the *Ornithischia*, or 'bird-hipped' dinosaurs."

David Lambert, *A Field Guide to Dinosaurs* (New York: Avon Books, 1983), p. 17. "Dinosaur features: Many of these features also occur in close relatives of the dinosaurs. A. Skull with 'windows' (closed in some dinosaurs), notably one in front of each eye. B. From two to 11 (fused) sacral vertebrae joining spine to: C. hip girdle with a hole (not found in other reptiles) — its strong upper rim helped this socket to take the: D. inturned top of the (fairly straight) thigh bone. E. Flange to anchor muscles aiding backswing of the leg. F. Ridge aiding knee extension. G. High, stiff, simple ankle. H. Dinosaurs walked on tiptoe. I. From three to five clawed or hoofed toes. J. From two to five clawed or hoofed fingers. K. Crest on upper arm bone aiding backswing of the forelimb. L. Shoulder socket angled to restrict forelimb movements to to-and-fro. M. Skin smooth or scaly, sometimes with horny armour."

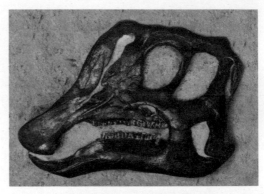

Hadrosaur Skull

Norell et.al., *Discovering Dinosaurs in the American Museum of Natural History,* p. 2. "Popularly, 'dinosaur' means any giant extinct 'monster,' especially ones that are ugly, stupid, and ill-suited to their environment, or anything else that is out-of-date. Scientifically, the group called dinosaurs must be defined in terms of evolution. This group must include all the animals descended from the first dinosaur, the common ancestor. Because the fossil record is incomplete and does not preserve all animals that have lived in the past, we will probably never find and identify the ancestor of all the dinosaurs. Nonetheless, we can recognize all the members of the group by identifying the unique evolutionary characteristics that they inherited from the first dinosaur."

David Norman, *The Illustrated Encyclopedia of Dinosaurs* (London: Salamander Books Limited, 1985), p. 9. "Dinosaurs lived during the so-called Mesozoic Era of earth history . . . thus animals that lived either before or after the Mesozoic are not dinosaurs. For example, giant wooly mammoths which went extinct within the last million years or so are not dinosaurs, nor are the large sail-backed reptiles of the Permian Period such as *Dimetrodon*. Dinosaurs are also reptiles. . . . To be even more precise, dinosaurs were a rather special group of reptiles. All of them were land-living creatures. . . . Thus the gigantic sea monsters of the Mesozoic, the *plesiosaurs*, *ichthyosaurs* and *mosasaurs* were not dinosaurs. Similarly no dinosaurs were airborne fliers, so . . . flying reptiles of the Mesozoic, the *pterosaurs*, were not dinosaurs. Dinosaurs are in fact members of a group of reptiles known as *archosaurs* ('ruling reptiles'), which include well-known creatures like crocodiles, the extinct *pterosaurs*, and those well-known *archosaur* descendants, the birds. . . . The dinosaurs are distinct from other *archosaurs* from one main reason which is . . . that they are able to walk and run extremely efficiently; their legs are tucked in beneath the body rather than being held out from the sides."

Merriam-Webster's Collegiate Dictionary, Tenth Edition (Springfield, MA: Merriam-Webster Inc., 1995), p. 326. Dinosaur "1: any of a group (*Dinosauria*) of extinct chiefly terrestrial carnivorous or herbivorous reptiles of the Mesozoic era. 2: any of various large extinct reptiles other than true dinosaurs."

12 Steven A. Austin, *Grand Canyon: Monument to Catastrophe* (El Cajon, CA: Institute for Creation Research,

1994), p. 111–131. Chapter 6, "Are Grand Canyon Rocks One Billion Years Old?" This chapter discusses the various methods of dating volcanic rocks and how it applied to the different basalt layers and sills found in the Grand Canyon. Page 126 lists the various dates achieved for these different layers. The Diabase Sills are found the deepest in the rock layers. The Cardenas Basalt is a Precambrian layer found at the bottom of the Grand Canyon and the basaltic rocks of the Uinkaret Plateau are found on top of the Grand Canyon. The Diabase Sills had dates ranging from 850 to 1370 million years; the Cardenas Basalt had dates that ranged from 715 to 1,100 million years and the basalt from the Uinkaret Plateau had dates that ranged from 0.01 to 2,600 million years. The basalt on the top could have been only 10,000 years old or as much as 2.6 billion years old, twice as old as the Cardenas Basalt found at the bottom of the Grand Canyon.

Henry M. Morris and John D. Morris, *Science, Scripture, and the Young Earth* (El Cajon, CA: Institute for Creation Research, 1989), p. 39–44. Chapter 8, "Bad Assumptions in Radiometric Dating." This chapter discusses the various assumptions made when using various methods of radiometric dating. Page 39 lists three basic and major assumptions as follows: ". . . all such methods require three fundamental assumptions: (1) constant half-life; (2) isolated system; (3) known initial conditions. None of these assumptions can be proved correct, or even be tested."

John D. Morris, *The Young Earth* (Green Forest, AR: Master Books, 1996), p. 51–67. Chapter 5, "Radioisotope Dating." This chapter discusses the many problems with radioisotope dating methods and the assumptions associated with them. "Certainly many people think radioisotope dating has proved that the earth is billions of years old and that this family of dating methods can determine the age of ancient rocks. However . . . the concepts suffer from various problems and unprovable assumptions. It must be stated before we begin to look at these methods, that the only rocks which can be dated by this method are igneous and metamorphic rocks, rocks which once were extremely hot and which since have cooled into solid rock. This would include rocks such as basalt (a type of solidified lava), rocks which are now quite hard, but once were in a hot, liquid, or semi-liquid condition. . . . Generally speaking, sedimentary rocks, such as limestone, sandstone, and shale, cannot be dated with radioisotope schemes. . . . Assumptions of Radioisotope Dating – 1. Constant decay rate. 2. No loss or gain of parent or daughter. 3. Known amounts of daughter present at start." It should be noted here that the vast majority of fossils are found in sedimentary rock and yet this is the only type of rock that even their flawed dating systems cannot date, leaving one to wonder just how do they get such exact dates on all of the fossils.

Ian T. Taylor, *In the Minds of Men* (Toronto: TFE Pub., 1984), p. 295–304. In chapter 11, "The Age of the Earth," Taylor describes the various methods of radioisotope dating including uranium/lead, potassium/argon, rubidium/strontium and lead/lead. Page 301 states: "The Assumptions of Radiometric Dating. 1. It is assumed that the earth began as a spinning blob of hot liquid that cooled to form the original rock surface. It is further assumed that, because of the immense span of time during which erosion and rebuilding are believed to have taken place, none of the original crustal materials are now available for study. 2. It is assumed that the crystals that are selected for radiometric age determination have been formed either by growing from hot liquid, that is, igneous rock, or by metamorphosis. . . . 3. Once the crystal has formed, it is assumed that it is a closed system, that is, no 'parent' or 'daughter' elements enter or leave the crystal lattice; the only change that takes place is assumed to be decay of the unstable 'parent' with time and consequent increase of the stable 'daughter' element. 4. When discordant results are obtained from processes operating within the same crystal, it is assumed that there has been loss or addition of the 'daughter' product. . . . 5. Contamination of the crystal during its formation by extraneous 'daughter' elements has to be taken into account, and it is assumed that the various isotope ratios of the contaminating element were the same at the time of crystal formation as they are today. 6. It is assumed that the decay 'constant,' determined over a two- or three-day period and mathematically related to the rate of decay expressed as half-life, has remained unchanged throughout the entire age of the mineral sample."

13 Dennis L. Breo, "Hunting Dino DNA — Mary Schweitzer Puts *T. rex* Bones Under the Microscope," *JAMA,* Vol. 270, No. 19, Nov. 17, 1993, p. 2376–2377. This article describes not only Mary Schweitzer's "addiction" to dinosaurs and her studies at the University of Montana under Jack Horner, but it also discusses her finds of red blood cells and DNA in the femur of a *T. rex*. She dates the fossil at 65 million years for no apparent reason other than perhaps based upon the belief that they became extinct then. Interestingly, when she talks about the DNA found in

T. rex

the bones, she says, "The DNA we've extracted from the *T. rex* bones may have come from a fungus that invaded the *T. rex* 65 million years ago; from a fungus that invaded the bones 5 years ago; from something else foreign like sagebrush root hairs; and, yes, from the blood of the *T. rex* itself." In other words, they really have no idea how old the DNA is or from where it came. This article concludes with a very interesting point, "Dinosaurs were so big and were around so long and, yet, we know almost nothing about them. They're magic." She's right! They really do know very little about them because they study them while wearing blinders to any and all evidence that does not fit into their evolutionary world view.

Mary Schweitzer and Tracy Staedter, "The Real Jurassic Park," *Earth*, June 1997, p. 55. "Finding remnants of dinosaur blood cells would have astounding implications. Tiny bits of proteins and DNA possibly locked away inside the structures could contain the coded message of life just waiting for scientists to decipher them. Recently, the notion of finding preserved dino DNA has produced a lot of headlines, not to mention blockbuster movies. Most scientists don't put much stock in the idea because it's unlikely that DNA could last for millions of years."

14 Don Batten, "Buddy Davis — The Creation Music Man (Who Makes Dinosaurs)," *Creation ex nihilo*, Vol. 19(3), 1997, p. 49. "You don't need to be a rocket scientist to figure the importance of this (finding thousands of fresh dinosaur bones in Alaska). To believe that it is 65 million years or more since these dinosaurs lived on earth — that takes a lot of faith. It doesn't take near as much faith to believe that they might have been frozen for a couple of thousand years at the most."

K. Davies, *Journal of Paleontology*, Vol. 61(1), p. 198–200. Geological Society of America abstract proceedings 17:548.

Margaret Helder, "Fresh Dinosaur Bones Found," *Creation ex nihilo,* Vol. 14(3), 1992, p. 16–17. "She could not accept that fresh (not permineralized, meaning unfossilized) dinosaur bones had been found in Alaska. Such bones could never have lasted 70 million years, she said. Unlikely or not, it is a fact that such bones have been found. . . . How these bones could have remained in fresh condition for 70 million years is a perplexing question. One thing is certain: they were not preserved by cold. Everyone recognizes that the climate in these regions was much warmer during the time when the dinosaurs lived. . . . Why then did these bones not decay long ago? . . . The obvious conclusion is that these bones were deposited in relatively recent times."

Philip J. Currie and Kevin Padian, editors, *The Encyclopedia of Dinosaurs,* "Jurassic Park," by Mary Schweitzer and Don Lessem (San Diego, CA: Academic Press, 1997), p. 385. "One of the first premises of the movie [*Jurassic Park*] is that DNA, the 'molecule of life' that codes the genetic composition of living organisms, can be preserved for 65–100 million years. There have been reports of DNA recovered from extinct organisms, such as the woolly mammoth or the horse-like quagga, but these specimens are not truly 'old' in a geological sense. DNA has been reported to have been recovered from specimens of millions of years old, but all of these reports still await independent verification. Whether DNA can be preserved for millions of years is still an issue very much open to debate and has by no means been accepted by the general scientific community."

Carl Wieland, "Sensational Dinosaur Blood Report," *Creation ex nihilo.* Vol. 19(4), 1997, p. 42–43. "To find unfossilized dinosaur bones is already an indication more consistent with a young age for the fossils. . . . The evidence that hemoglobin has indeed survived in this dinosaur bone (which casts immense doubt upon the 'millions of years' idea) is, to date, as follows: • The tissue was coloured reddish brown, the colour of hemoglobin, as was liquid extracted from the dinosaur tissue. • Hemoglobin contains heme units. Chemical signatures unique to heme were found in the specimens when certain wave lengths of laser light were applied. • Because it contains iron, heme reacts to magnetic fields differently from other proteins — extracts from this specimen reacted in the same way as modern heme compounds. • To ensure that the samples had not been contaminated with certain bacteria which have heme (but never the protein hemoglobin), extracts of the dinosaur fossil were injected over several weeks into rats. If there was even a minute amount of hemoglobin present in the *T. rex* sample, the rats' immune system should build up detectable antibodies against this compound. This is exactly what happened in carefully controlled experiments. Evidence of hemoglobin, and the still-recognizable shapes of red blood cells in unfossilized dinosaur bone is powerful testimony against the whole idea of dinosaurs living millions of years ago."

Nigel Williams, "The Trials and Tribulations of Cracking the Prehistoric Code," *Science*, Vol. 269, August 18, 1995, p. 923–924. "One of the key questions researchers are still grappling with is just how long DNA can survive. Biochemist Thomas Lindahl of Britain's Imperial Cancer Research Fund at South Mimms has studied the main mechanisms that degrade DNA — hydrolysis and the loss of purines, one of the chemical building blocks of the molecule. He has found that, by the standards of most biological molecules, DNA can be remarkably long-lived. 'Results of ancient DNA up to 50,000 to 100,000 years old are credible,' he says, adding that beyond this time it is much harder to envision how the molecule could be protected from decay, as even encased in materials such as amber, oxidative damage would be expected. Lindahl believes researchers claiming to have older DNA should explain how it was preserved."

15 Schweitzer and Staedter, "The Real Jurassic Park," p. 55–57. This article describes the process of finding the red blood cells within the thin sections of the unfossilized inner section of the T. rex femur, and how they believe it to be improbable that it really is blood cells as this quote from page 55 indicates, "So I showed these microscopic slides to my boss, paleontologist Jack Horner, renowned for his work on dinosaur nesting sites. He took a long look and then asked, 'So you think these are red blood cells?' I said, 'No.' He said, 'Well, prove that they're not.' So far, we haven't been able to."

16 John R. Horner and Edwin Dobb, *Dinosaur Lives* (New York: Harper Collins Publishers, 1997), p. 228.

17 Batten, "Buddy Davis: the Creation Music Man," p. 49. "Buddy, you recently had a visit to Alaska to find 'fresh' dinosaur bones — can you tell us about that?"

"Sure, Our team of five went to the North Slope of Alaska, about as far north as you can go without actually getting into the Arctic Ocean . . . the third day we found our first dinosaur remains. . . . The Liscomb Bone Bed has probably thousands of frozen unfossilized dinosaur bones — some of them have the ligaments still attached."

Margaret Helder, "Fresh Dinosaur Bones Found," *Creation ex nihilo*, Vol. 14(3), 1992, p. 16. "In 1961, a petroleum geologist discovered a large, half-meter-thick bone bed. As the bones were fresh, not permineralized, he assumed that these were recent bison bones. It took 20 years for scientists to recognize duckbill dinosaur bones in this deposit as well as the bones of horned dinosaurs, and large and small carnivorous dinosaurs."

18 Associated Press, "Gout Also a Big Pain for Dinosaurs," *Cincinnati Enquirer*, May, 23, 1997. This article was notifying the general public about an article being published in the journal called *Nature* that discussed the dis-

covery that "Sue," a *T. rex* skeleton found in 1990 apparently suffered from gout. The article from *Nature* is referenced below in this same endnote.

Horner and Lessem, *The Complete T. rex*, p. 71-2. (Referring to the largest *T. rex* found to date) "Sue's skull is in terrific shape, black teeth still in massive jaws that aren't distorted. And her bones show all sorts of injuries that had healed over in the course of what must have been a long, rough life. Extra bone growth along the lower left shin indicates to Pete Larson that Sue had a broken leg that healed over, though it might also have suffered from osteoporosis, arthritis, or other bone diseases that we know dinosaurs had. There is a hole that might have been a drain for a cheek infection. There are parallel grooves along the pelvis, maybe from the raking bite or slash of another *T. rex*. Two vertebrae near the end of the tail were probably broken. They were found fused with extra bone around them. There is a rib incompletely healed from a fracture. And there is a tooth still embedded in a rib, from a bite by another *T. rex* (which may have come after Sue's death)."

Lessem and Glut, *The Dinosaur Society's Dinosaur Encyclopedia*, p. viii. "Deformed, fractured, and healed bones inform us about dinosaur diseases."

Malcolm W. Moran, "Dinosaur May Have Suffered from Gout," *Denver Post*, May, 22 1997. "The scientists who examined some of the dinosaur's bones have concluded that the equivalent of hand bones (metacarpals) at the ends of the animal's spindly forearm are riddled with lesions strikingly similar to those observed in some modern animals — birds, reptiles, and humans, for example — suffering from gout. Gout is a metabolic disease, in which uric acid erodes bone tissues and deposits sharp mineral crystal in joints, causing excruciating pain. Earlier studies had found that Sue's facial bones had been slashed by deep gashes, a dinosaur tooth was left embedded in one of her ribs, and she probably limped from a badly healed broken leg. 'Sue was not a well dinosaur.' "

Bruce M. Rothschild, Darren Tanke, and Ken Carpenter, "Tyrannosaurs Suffered from Gout," *Nature*, Vol. 387, May 22, 1997, p. 357. "Gout is a metabolic disorder in which urate crystals accumulate as space-occupying masses, producing monarticular spheroidal erosions in bone, often associated with new bone growth at their borders. We now report the first identification of such lesions in dinosaurs. Caricatures of the agony and ill-temper of those afflicted with gout are magnified by its recognition in *Tyrannosaurs rex*." The article continues on, describing in detail the lesions found on the bones.

Sothebys, "Sue: The Tyrannosaurus Rex," 1997, http://www.sothebys.com/sue_trex/homejs.html "In addition to the near pristine state of preservation, the most intriguing aspect of "Sue" is the number of evident pathologies displayed by the bones: a broken and healed left fibula, broken and healed ribs, broken and healed tail bones, bite and puncture marks on the left side of the skull, and muscle reattachment to the right humerus.

19 Romans 5:12–14. "Wherefore, as by one man sin entered into the world, and death by sin; and so death passed upon all men, for that all have sinned. . . . Nevertheless death reigned from Adam to Moses, even over them that had not sinned after the similitude of Adam's transgression, who is the figure of him that was to come."

1 Corinthians 15:21–22. "For since by man came death, by man came also the resurrection of the dead. For as in Adam all die, even so in Christ shall all be made alive."

James Stambaugh, "Creation and the Problem of Evil," unpublished paper presented at the Evangelical Theological Society's National Meeting in Philadelphia, PA, Nov. 17, 1995. A copy of this paper is on file at the office of Answers in Genesis. This paper discusses several

**Jesus
Christ
"The Last
Adam"**
1 Cor. 15:45

For as in Adam all die,
even so in Christ shall all be made alive
1 Cor. 15:22

**"The
First
Adam"**
1 Cor. 15:45

aspects of the problem of evil, including suffering. The
following is taken from the Abstract of this paper: "The
problem of evil continues to be a supposed 'safe haven'
for the skeptic. He believes that issue gives evidence to
support his rebellious attitude toward Christianity. Un-
fortunately, many evangelicals, by adopting theistic evolution, give credence to the skeptic's argument."
James Stambaugh, "Creation and the Curse," unpublished
paper presented at the Evangelical Theological Society's
Far West Region Meeting, The Master's Seminary, Sun
Valley, California, April 26, 1996. A copy of this paper
is on file at the office of Answers in Genesis. This paper

addresses the subject of the Curse and its affect on creation and in so doing, examines Romans 8:19–21.

Stambaugh, "Creation, Suffering and the Problem of Evil." This paper explains how at the end of the sixth day of creation, God called His entire creation "very good," meaning that there could not have been any form of suffering or evil.

20 Lambert and the Diagram Group, *The Dinosaur Data Book*, p. 197. "Skin impressions: Some dinosaur skins left their impressions in fine-grained sediments that later hardened into rocks." (Illustration on page): "Impressions left by a duck-billed dinosaur's leathery skin with horny tubercles that formed a raised pebbled pattern. *Hadrosaur* skin impression includes clustered larger bumps that might have had distinctive colors. Some *Hadrosaurs* had rows of big bumps on the hips and belly."

Teresa Lambright, "The Find of a Lifetime," *Carlsbad Current-Argus*, February 28, 1997. "Researchers had determined the pockmarked rock is actually the 70-million-year-old fossilized skin of a duck-billed dinosaur. Since then, the find has been hailed nationally as one of only a dozen impressions of duck-billed dinosaur skin discovered worldwide. . . . I thought, *Wow, this is a skin impression*, he said, remembering the first signs of the ten-foot by two-foot stone."

Lessem and Glut, *The Dinosaur Society's Dinosaur Encyclopedia*, p. viii. "Rare skin impressions in fine-grained rock show the patterns of dinosaur scales. The even rarer dinosaur mummies have preserved fragments of the soft tissue, allowing us to reconstruct with considerable confidence what dinosaurs looked like when they were alive."

Norell et al., *Discovering Dinosaurs in the American Museum of Natural History*, p. 26-28. "Only a few dinosaur specimens preserved under these special conditions have been discovered and in rare cases skin impressions are

CREATIONWISE

preserved. The most spectacular of these specimens is the Museum's *Edmontosaurus* mummy. This specimen preserves impressions of skin over almost the entire body. . . . Several other specimens in the Museum's collection have fossilized skin impressions."

Jake Schoellkopf, "Skin Deep," *The Sydney Morning Herald*, April 20, 1996. "Skin deep. . . . Spencer Lucas, the curator of paleontology at the Museum of Natural History in Albuquerque, New Mexico, with the cast of a 70-million-year-old fossilized dinosaur skin which the museum is inviting visitors to stroke."

21 Susan West, "Dinosaur Head Hunt," *Science News*, Vol.

116(18), Nov. 3, 1979, p. 314-5. "The new skull also throws *Brontosaurus* into a different classification. *Brontosaurus* is a member of the suborder *Sauropoda*, the largest four-legged creatures ever to shake the earth. The skull it sported this last century or so placed it in the same family as the less spectacular and quite different sauropod *Camarasaurus*. Its new head puts it in the same family as its nearly identical cousin, *Diplodocus*."

22 Lambert and the Diagram Group, *The Dinosaur Data Book*, p. 26–27. This diagram shows that around 240 to 230 million years ago (according to their time frame), there are NO filled in branches in the family tree of the dinosaurs. Had this been a real tree, there would be nothing more than a bunch of loose twigs on the ground.

Norman, *The Illustrated Encyclopedia of Dinosaurs*, p. 20–23. These pages discuss the family trees of the animals believed to have preceded the dinosaurs and then it shows a tree for the dinosaurs themselves. As with the example above, the period around 230 million years has absolutely NO connections to any of the branches, just hypothetical lines. In real life, you would not have a tree, but instead a nice pile of firewood.

23 James Stambaugh, "The Days of Creation: A Semantic Approach." *Creation ex nihilo Technical Journal*, Vol. 5, No. 1. 1991, p. 70–78. This paper conducts an in-depth study into the Hebrew word for day, *yôm* and clearly shows how it can mean nothing more nor less than a literal 24-hour day.

24 Morris, *The Genesis Record*, p. 42–46. Morris discusses a number of the chronological works that have been carried out to determine the date of creation. Page 45 gives the following lists of dates: "In addition to Ussher's date of 4004 B.C. for the creation, many other dates have been computed, some of which are as follows (all in years B.C.) : Jewish, 3760; Septuagint, 5270; Josephus, 5555; Kepler, 3993; Melanchthon, 3964; Luther, 3961;

Lightfoot, 3960; Hales, 5402; Playfair, 4008; Lipman, 3916; and others. . . . Consequently, the account of earth history as recorded in Genesis fixes the creation of the universe at several thousand, rather than several billion, years ago. The exact date may be as long ago as 10,000 B.C., or as recently as 4000 B.C., with the probabilities (from biblical considerations, at least) favoring the lower end of this spectrum."

Taylor, *In the Minds of Men*, p. 282–308. Chapter 11 — "The Age of the Earth." This chapter discussed not only the biblical chronology of the earth, but also delves into various areas of science including salt in the sea, Israel's chronometer, cooling of the earth, and Lord Kelvin and the principles of radiometric dating. The following statement from page 283 gives a clear indication that the problem with an old earth really did not surface till after Lyell and Darwin. "The Age of the Earth Before Lyell and Darwin — One concise and readily available source of nineteenth century information is Robert Young's concordance, and in the popular twenty-second edition, under 'creation,' will be found a list of thirty-seven computations of the date of creation from a possible list of more than one hundred and twenty. Of these thirty-seven, thirty are based on the Bible and seven are derived from other sources — Abyssinian, Arab,

Pachycephalosaurus

Babylonian, Chinese, Egyptian, Indian, and Persian. Not one of these ancient records puts the date of creation earlier than 7000 B.C. In all the hundreds of thousands of years over which hominid man is alleged to have evolved, it is surely more than coincidental that ancient civilizations, which were by no means ignorant of time-keeping by astronomical methods, should all begin their historical record at this arbitrary date. In addition, all the myths and legends, however bizarre, speak of instant creation just a few thousand years earlier."

Ussher, *The Annals of the World*. At the time of this writing, a close friend, Larry Pierce, is translating Ussher's works from the Latin into English. Larry has been amazed at the detail and accuracy of Ussher's work and is thoroughly convinced of his date of 4004 B.C. ± just a few years, for the creation of the universe.

25 Benton, *Dinosaurs: An A-Z Guide*, p. 14. "In 1677, Dr. Robert Plot gave the first description of a dinosaur. In his book *The Natural History of Oxfordshire* he included a drawing of the end of a thighbone of *Megalosaurus*: he said it was from a giant man."

Michael Benton, *Dinosaur and Other Prehistoric Animal Fact Finder* (New York: Kingfisher Books, 1992), p. 8–9. "The first large bone to be reported from Europe was part of the leg bone of a dinosaur found near Oxford, England. In his book *The Natural History of Oxfordshire*, published in 1677, Robert Plot of Oxford University described the bone as that of an elephant or a giant human, although he was not very sure of these identifications."

Norell et.al., *Discovering Dinosaurs in the American Museum of Natural History*, p. 6. "In northern Europe, Robert Plot made the first unmistakable reference to dinosaur bones in 1677. Plot described the lower end of the thigh bone that formed the knee of *Megalosaurus*, a bipedal carnivorous dinosaur common in the Jurassic rocks of southern England."

John Noble Wilford, *The Riddle of the Dinosaur* (New York: Alfred A Knopf, 1985), p. 33–34. "Earlier fossil collectors, as might be expected, had found *megalosaur* bones without knowing their significance. A 'human thigh-bone' from Oxfordshire was described in 1677 by the Rev. Robert Plot, first keeper of the Ashmolean Museum at Oxford. It was actually the lower end of a dinosaur thigh, probably from a *Megalosaur.*"

26 Norman, *The Illustrated Encyclopedia of Dinosaurs*, p. 10. "*Scrotum humanum* was the caption provided for this piece of bone by R. Brooks in 1763. It was first illustrated by Robert Plot in 1676 who thought it belonged to a giant human. Though now lost, it may have been the lower end of the thigh bone of *Megalosaurus.*"

27 Benton, *Dinosaur and Other Prehistoric Animal Fact Finder*, p. 10. "The second dinosaur to be named came from Lewes in Sussex, England. It was discovered by Mary Ann Mantell in 1822. She was out walking when she spotted an enormous fossil tooth in a pile of rubble beside the road. She showed the tooth to her husband, Dr. Gideon Mantell, a keen amateur fossil collector. He found more bones of the same animal nearby, and named it *Iguanodon* ("iguana tooth"), thinking that it was a giant iguana lizard."

Dixon et al., *The MacMillan Illustrated Encyclopedia of Dinosaurs and Prehistoric Animals,* p. 144. "*Iguanodon* rightly deserves its place in dinosaur lore. It was the second dinosaur to be discovered, although the word 'dinosaur' had yet to be invented. Part of this great shin bone was found in southern England in 1809, and then some teeth and other bones were discovered in 1819. Scientists of the day regarded the teeth as belonging to some giant mammal, like a rhinoceros. But Gideon Mantell, a geologist and keen fossil collector, saw that the teeth were reptilian, and that they resembled those of the modern iguana of Central and South America. So he named the animal *Iguanodon*, and described it in 1825 to the scientific community."

Lambert and the Diagram Group. *The Dinosaur Data Book*, p. 279. "Mantell, Gideon A. (1790–1852) British physician and fossil hunter who largely pioneered dinosaur discovery. He named *Iguanodon* (1825), *Hylaeosaurus* (1833), and *Pelorosaurus* (1850). *Iguanodon* was the second dinosaur to get a scientific name."

Wilford, *The Riddle of the Dinosaur*, p. 5, 35–44. "No genus survived through the entire Age of Reptiles, but dinosaurs of one kind or another flourished for 160 million years (humans may be 3 to 4 million years old, if the early hominids are counted), and then the last of them died off at the close of the Cretaceous." Chapter 2 – "Discovery of Time," p. 35–44 describes the history of the earth through the eyes of an evolutionist and places the dinosaurs some 62 million years before man.

28 Lambert and the Diagram Group. *The Dinosaur Data Book*, p. 279. "British physician and fossil hunter who largely pioneered dinosaur discovery."

29 Lambert and the Diagram Group. *The Dinosaur Data Book*, p. 289. "Contrary to comic books and motion pictures, no dinosaur survived to frighten early man 'one million years B.C.' Nor did all dinosaurs live at the same time."

Norman, *The Illustrated Encyclopedia of Dinosaurs*, p. 14. "Early man however did not appear on earth until a mere 2–3 million years ago — long after the dinosaurs went extinct!"

David Norman, *Dinosaur!* (New York: Macmillan, Inc., 1991), p. 23. "Most people now know that dinosaurs became extinct about 66 million years ago, because it is a subject which has received a considerable airing in the press, on television and the radio. . . . The whole issue of time is further confused today through television and films. The very popular cartoon series *The Flintstones* gives the clear impression that Stone Age man lived alongside dinosaurs, and even had some as pets! It is difficult to erase the mistaken ideas that such scenes create. The simple fact is that dinosaurs vanished from the face of the earth almost 66 million years before modern humans appeared. Our history dates back a mere 100,000 years, so any thoughts of cavemen wrestling with *Tyrannosaurus* are completely nonsense."

Wilford, *The Riddle of the Dinosaur*, p. 5, 35–44. "No genus survived through the entire Age of Reptiles, but dinosaurs of one kind or another flourished for 160 million years (humans may be 3 to 4 million years old, if the early hominids are counted), and then the last of them died off at the close of the Cretaceous." Chapter 2, "Discovery of Time," p. 35–44, describes the history of the earth through the eyes of an evolutionist and places the dinosaurs some 62 million years before man.

30 Edwin H. Colbert, *The Great Dinosaur Hunters and Their Discoveries* (New York: Dover Publications, Inc., 1984), p. 32. "For this group, Owen coined the name *Dinosauria* — from the Greek *deinos*, meaning terrible, and *sauros*, meaning lizard. (One must not be confused by Owen's choice of a Greek word meaning 'lizard' when he devised the name for this group of reptiles; the Greeks did not always have a word for everything, so Owen chose the term the etymologically which was the nearest this he could get. Perhaps it is permissible to extend the original meaning of the Greek word, and think of *sauros* in this connection as meaning 'reptile.') The name was proposed by Owen at the meeting of the British Association for the Advancement of Science, convened at Plymouth in 1841. It was published in 1842 in the proceedings of the association."

Dixon et al., *The MacMillan Illustrated Encyclopedia of Dinosaurs and Prehistoric Animals,* p. 90-2. "It was Sir Richard Owen, the great English anatomist who founded the British Museum of Natural History, who made this

Chasmosaurus

discovery and who, in 1841, coined the name Dinosauria for them, meaning 'terrible liz-- ards.'"

Feduccia, *The Origin and Evolution of Birds*, p. 26. "Richard Owen, the famed anatomist who at the age of thirty-eight had coined the term *Dinosauria*, was in fact not a creationist, as was popularly thought, but rather had a great disdain for Darwin's explanation of evolution by natural selection and was, as mentioned, at odds with 'Darwin's Bulldog,' Thomas Huxley."

Russell M. Grigg, "Dinosaurs and Dragons: Stamping on the Legends!" *Creation ex nihi lo*, Vol. 14(3), 1990, p. 11. "The stamps were released by the Royal Mail on August 20, 1991, to celebrate the 150th anniversary of the first use of the term *'dinosauria.'* "

31 Norman, *The Illustrated Encyclopedia of Dinosaurs*, p. 8. "Richard Owen (1804-1892), who first coined the term *Dinosauria*. A leading comparative anatomist, he became the first superintendent of the British Museum (Natural History)."

32 Norman, *The Illustrated Encyclopedia of Dinosaurs*, p. 8. "Comparisons that Owen was able to make at the time suggested to him that these peculiar reptiles, which he named dinosaurs after the Greek words *deinos* and *sauros* or 'terrible reptiles,' seemed to anticipate the form of the large pachydermal mammals of today."

Wilford, *The Riddle of the Dinosaur*, p. 57. "Owen coined the name from the Greek *deinos*, meaning 'terrible' or 'fear fully great,' and *sauros*, meaning 'lizard' — *Dinosauria*, terrible lizard. It is odd that he chose a word meaning lizard when he had in mind setting these creatures apart from lizards, but then he probably thought of *sauros* in the more general sense of 'reptile,' "

33 D. (Lee) Niermann, "Dinosaurs and Dragons," *Creation ex nihilo Technical Journal*, Vol. 8(1), 1994, p. 85–104. "In the West, dragons were described by body type and defined by habitat. In China, however, they were classified according to their purposes and functions." — (p. 89) "In 1611 B.C., the Emperor of China appointed the first Royal Dragon Feeder . . . [which] remained an honored post for years. . . . And as earlier mentioned, one of the Sung Dynasty emperors had a dragon reared in his palace compound." — (p. 100)

Paul Taylor, *The Great Dinosaur Mystery and the Bible* (Colorado Springs, CO: Chariot Family Publishing, 1989), p. 42. "Some old Chinese books even tell of a family that kept 'dragons' and raised the babies. It is said that in those days, Chinese kings used 'dragons' for pulling royal chariots on special occasions."

34 Bill Cooper, "The Early History of Man — Part 4. Living Dinosaurs from AngloSaxon and other Early Records," *Creation ex nihilo Technical Journal*, Vol.6(1), 1992, p. 49–66. This paper discussed the many legends of writings that describe the dragons and monsters of early European history. The following is from the Introduction to this paper: "There are, of course, the famous descriptions of two such monsters from the Old Testament, *Behemoth* and *Leviathan* (Job 40:15– 41:34), *Behemoth* being a giant vegetarian that lived on the fens, and *Leviathan*

Tylosaur skull

a somewhat more terrifying armour-plated amphibian whom only children and the most foolhardy would want as a pet. The Egyptians knew *Behemoth* by the name p'ih.mv, which is the same name, of course. *Leviathan* was similarly known as Lotan to the men of Ugarit. Babylonian and Sumerian literature has preserved details of similar creatures, as has the written and unwritten folklore of peoples around the world. But perhaps the most remarkable descriptions of living dinosaurs are those that the Anglo-Saxon and Celtic peoples of Europe have passed down to us."

Bill Cooper, *After the Flood* (West Sussex, England: New Wine Press, 1995). Chapter 10, "Dinosaurs from Anglo-Saxon and other Records," p. 130–145; Chapter 11, "Beowulf and the Creatures of Denmark," p. 146–161. Both of these chapters discuss the overwhelming evidence of dinosaurs or dinosaur-like creatures that are found throughout the early European history of the Anglo-Saxons and the Danish peoples. Included in the text are photos of early artwork that depicts the various creatures including one such picture on page 158 with the following description: "A most graphic portrayal from Saxon times of an attack on a herd of long-necked quadrupeds by a bipedal predator. Note the predator's two large legs and puny forearms. This portrayal conforms very closely indeed to the description of Grendel, and is

a clear indication that such creatures were to be seen on the British mainland as well as the Continent, as is

Corythosaurus

also shown by Athelstan's and other charters. The stone can be seen inside the church of SS. Mary and Hardulph at Breedon-on-the-Hill in Leicestershire."

Niermann, "Dinosaurs and Dragons," p. 85–104. This article also discusses the many legends and recorded sightings of creatures that are best described as dinosaurs, dragons, and pterosaurs from places such as France, Scandinavia, England, Ireland, Germany, Switzerland, Italy, Ukraine India, Phrygia, Poland, Draconum, Africa, and China.

Peter Wellnhofer, *Pterosaurs: The Illustrated Encyclopedia of Prehistoric Flying Reptiles* (New York: Barnes & Noble, 1991), p. 20–21. "If we pursue the history of the investigation of pterosaurs, the flying saurians of prehistoric times, there is a natural link in our minds with the myths and legends of dragons. These were usually also seen as winged lizards or snakes. For 16th and 17th century scholars dragons were still a reality. For example, in the *Schlangenbuch* (Snake Book) by the famous Swiss naturalist and town doctor Conrad Gessner, dating from 1589, there is a chapter called, 'Von den tracken,' in which he describes a battle between a Swiss called Winkelried and a dragon which took place near the Swiss village of Wyler. The scholarly Jesuit father Athanasius Kirsher provided a picture of this fight in his great work on natural history, *Mundus Subterraneus* (The World Below the Earth) in 1678. According to this, the dragon had a long neck and tail, four legs, and wings. . . . Even in the early seventeenth century such legends persisted, like that of the flying dragon on Mount Pilatus near Lucerne in Switzerland. It is reported that the creature flew out of a cave on Mount Pilatus in 1619, and flapped across the valley with slowly beating wings. . . . Ancient notions of dragons suggest they had a snake-like body, two legs and bat's wings. A second pair of legs was not added until the 16th century. These different types of dragons are impressively presented in Conrad Gessner's 1589 *Book of Snakes*. There are similar pictures in *Sebastianus Munsterus' Cosmographia Universa*, printed in Basel in 1544."

35 Paul Taylor, *The Great Dinosaur Mystery* (Mesa, AZ: Films for Christ, 1991).

36 Henry M. Morris, *The Biblical Basis for Modern Science* (Grand Rapids, MI: Baker Book House, 1984), p. 351. "Dragons, for example (Hebrew *tannim*), are mentioned at least twenty-five times in the Old Testament. In one of these, the word is used synonymously with 'leviathan that crooked serpent,' being called 'the dragon that is in the sea' (Isa. 27:1). Ezekiel 27:3 refers to 'the great dragon that lieth in the midst of his [that is, Egypt's] rivers.' On the other hand, the mountains of Edom are said to have been laid 'waste for the dragons of the wilderness' (Mal. 1:3)."

James Strong, *The New Strong's Exhaustive Concordance of the Bible* (Nashville, TN: Thomas Nelson Pub., 1984), p. 289. Dragon(s) *tannim*, #8577 used 21 times in the King James Version Old Testament.

Robert Young, *Young's Analytical Concordance to the Bible* (Peabody, MA: Hendrickson Publishers, 1996), p. 270. Dragon(s) *tannim*, used 21 times in the Old Testament.

37 As the term "dinosaur" technically refers to creatures that lived on the land, the "dragons" that lived in the sea would not technically be dinosaurs — but one could refer to them as "dinosaur-like" creatures.

38 Sylvia J. Czerkas and Stephen A. Czerkas, *Dinosaurs: A Global View* (Spain: Barnes & Noble Books, 1996), p. 179. "With a skull as much as 3 m (10 ft) in length, *Kronosaurus* existed within shallow seas which covered what is now central Australia. It was one of the short-necked pliosaurs, and was among the largest of marine reptiles. The feeding behavior of *Kronosaurus* was probably similar to that of Orca, the killer whale, in that they

fed upon sizable prey. *Kronosaurus* reached lengths of approximately 14 m (45 ft)."

Dixon et al., *The MacMillan Illustrated Encyclopedia of Dinosaurs and Prehistoric Animals,* p. 77. "Name: *Kronosaurus*, Time: Early Cretaceous, Locality: Australia (Queensland). Size: 42 ft./12.8 m long. The Australia *Kronosaurus* is the largest-known pliosaur. Its skull was flat-topped and massively long, measuring 9 ft./2.7 m — almost a quarter of the total body length, and therefore substantially larger and more powerful than that of the greatest carnivorous dinosaur, *Tyrannosaurus.*"

Norman, *The Illustrated Encyclopedia of Dinosaurs*, p. 179. "Short-necked or 'pliosauroid' plesiosaurs seem to have been more like the killer whales of today. Powerfully built with enormous heads — one particularly large pliosauroid, *Kronosaurus* ('time reptile') from Queensland, Australia, has a head nearly 8 ft. (2.4 m) long — these animals must have been formidable predators of most aquatic creatures including other plesiosaurs, ichthyosaurs (if it could catch them!), giant turtles, and large ammonites."

Rhamphorhynchus

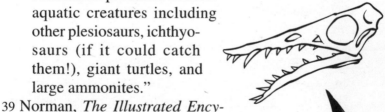

39 Norman, *The Illustrated Encyclopedia of Dinosaurs,* p. 170–172. Describes various pterosaurs including the *Pteranodon* and *Rhamphorhynchus. Pteranodon* means "winged and toothless" and *Rhamphorhynchus* means "narrow beak."

Wellnhofer, *Pterosaurs: The Illustrated Encyclopedia of Prehistoric Flying Reptiles*, p. 83–85, 135–136. "The most frequently occurring genus is *Rhamphorhynchus*

(=beak-snout), a long-tailed pterosaur after whom the whole suborder is named *Rhamphorhynchoidea*. . . . So far five different species of this genus have been found in Solnhofen. The smallest, *Rhamphorhynchus longicaudus* has a skull only 1.18 in. long (3 cm) and a wing span of 15.75 in. (40 cm). The largest species, *Rhamphorhynchus longiceps*, has a skull 7.5 in. (19 cm) long, a wing span of 5.74 ft. (1.75 m). . . . *Pteranodon ingens* had a skull 5.9 ft. (1.79 m) long, of which almost half consisted of the crest, rising well back over the rump. *Pteranodon sternbergi* had a crest which rose steeply and was broader at the top. The lower jaw alone of this species is 3.9 ft. (1.2 m) long, thus longer by a third than *Pteranodon ingens*, which had an estimated wing span of about 23 ft. (7 m). *Pteranodon sternbergi* was thus one of the largest known pterosaurs, and must have had a wing span of over 30 ft. (9 m)."

40 Spencer G. Lucas, *Dinosaurs — The Textbook* (Dubuque, IA: Wm. C. Brown Publishers, 1994), p. 194–196. "The term coprolite, from the Greek roots *copros* (feces) and *lithos* (rock), is applied to fossilized feces. . . . They provide paleontologists with direct evidence of an extinct animal's diet. But their use is greatly limited because we are unable, except in rare cases, to link confidently a given coprolite to the animal that produced it. This limitation especially affects dinosaurs. Few bona fide dinosaur coprolites have been identified, and there has been little analysis of them. . . . At present, few dinosaur coprolites have been identified, and little analysis of them has been undertaken. This means that collecting and studying dinosaur coprolites remains a largely untapped

Pteranodon

field of research that may teach us more about the behavior and diets of dinosaurs."

41 Benton, *Dinosaur and Other Prehistoric Animal Fact Finder*, p. 105. *Estemmenosuchus* — "This giant Russian form had long sharp front teeth, buttony cheek teeth behind, which shows that it ate plants."

Dave Marrs and Virginia Kylberg, *Dino Cards*, 1991. *Estemmenosuchus* was a large mammal-like reptile. "Despite having menacing-looking fangs it apparently was a plant-eater."

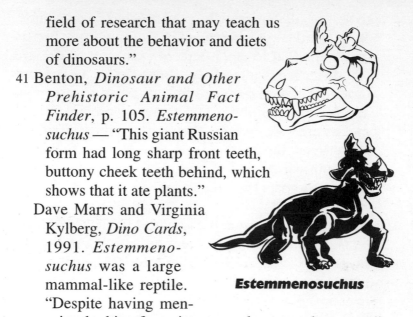

Estemmenosuchus

42 Kathleen Brandes, *Vanishing Species* (New York: Time-Life Books, 1974), p. 98. Concerning the giant panda: "Although classified among the carnivores because of common ancestry, pandas live mainly on enormous amounts of bamboo."

Keith and Liz Laidler, *Pandas: Giants of the Bamboo Forest* (London: BBC Books, 1992), p. 80–81. "But it is the structure of the skull and jaw that the pandas reveal the most obvious adaptations to a bamboo diet. Any animal that needs to eat large amounts of hard-stemmed vegetation needs three special talents: strong teeth, strong jaws, and enough muscle-power to use them. . . . The giant panda's jaw is extremely heavy boned, much heavier than that of a bear, the carnivore it most closely resembles, and carries teeth which, while fitting the general carnivore 'blueprint,' show heavy modification for a herbivorous diet. . . . Most carnivores have carnissial teeth, modified premolars shaped like blades, which act as shears, allowing the animals to scissor off lumps of its prey neatly and efficiently. Both pandas and bears, whose omnivorous diet is made up of at least 75 percent plant material, have lost their carnassial teeth. . . . Both the premolars and molar teeth have been strongly modified for crushing and grinding bamboo. The posterior premolars and molars are wide and flat, their surfaces heavily ridged and cusped; the panda's teeth appear, superficially at least, more like those of cud-chewing species such as cattle and goats than the carnivore from which they evolved."

43 Maria Pia Mannucci and Alessandro Minelli, *Great Book of the Animal Kingdom* (New York, NY: Arch Cape Press, 1988), p. 242–243. Flying foxes are only found in the tropics and sub-tropics of the Old World. Their distribution is limited by the fact that they need to find fruit all year round. . . . Indian flying foxes live mainly on the juice of ripe fruit. The bats fly silently into the food trees and clamber along the branches to the fruit. They pull the thin branches toward them with their thumb claws and seize the fruit with the four big, sharp canine teeth. . . . Flying foxes feed on a large number of tropical fruits, such as bananas, mangoes, guavas, and figs. They squeeze the juice from them and then spit out the tough fiber.

44 William Ashworth and Art Wolf, *Bears: Their Life and Behaviour* (New York: Crown Publishers, Inc., 1992), p. 21. "Carnivore means 'meat-eater,' and that is what dogs generally are. Bears are not. Like us, bears are omnivores, which means that they will eat just about anything in sight. Most of what is in sight is plants, so most of what bears eat is plant matter. What we have here, it turns out, are the largest, fiercest vegetarians on the planet."

Macdonald, *The Encyclopedia of Mammals*, p. 89. "Grizzlies cannot digest fibrous vegetation well and they are highly selective feeders. The diet shows shifts as they move from alpine meadows to salmon streams to avalanche chutes and riverside brushlands. Grizzlies are omnivorous, with flattened cheek teeth and piercing canines 30 mm (1.2 in.) or more in length. Their large claws often exceed 6 cm (2.4 in.) in length; they are used to dig up tubers and burrowing rodents. The diet is dominated by vegetation, primarily succulent herbage, tubers and berries." p. 96 "The Spectacled bear of South America . . . is a good climber, commonly foraging in trees in search of succulent bromeliad 'hearts,' petioles of palm fronds, and fruits such as figs in the forest and cactus in the desert. . . . Although primarily herbivorous, the Spectacled bear also feeds on insects, carrion, occasionally domestic stock, and reportedly young deer, guanacos and vicunas." p. 96 "The Sun bear or Malayan sun bear . . . is omnivorous, eating tree fruits, succulent growing tips of palm trees, termites, small mammals and birds, and can cause significant damage in cocoa and coconut plantations." p. 97 "The Asian black bear . . . is omnivorous, feeding mainly on plant material, especially nuts and fruit, but also ants and larvae. It is a good climber and frequently forages in trees and on succulent vegetation on avalanche slopes."

Maria Pia Mannucci and Alessandro Minelli, *Great Book of the Animal Kingdom* (New York: Arch Cape Press, 1988), p. 285–287. When describing the brown bear: "They are basically herbivorous, although they will eat animal matter if they get the chance. In early spring and summer green plants such as grasses, sedges, and shoots make up the most important part of their diet. In certain regions bears are quite happy to eat the roots of herbaceous plants. During the late summer and fall, when the bear is building up its reserves of fat for the winter, berries and nuts, such as rowan berries, bilberries, hazel nuts, beechmast, and acorns, become important. . . . Brown bears do not appear to be particularly fond of the flesh of vertebrates and they only prey on wild ungulates in certain circumstances." When describing black bears: "The American black bear's diet is similar to the brown bear's but it is more markedly herbivorous. Depending on the season and the environment, plant matter forms between 85 and 98 percent of its diet. During the spring (April–May) American black bears feed mainly on grasses. In June they add insects to their diet, and in the fall their main sources of food are berries, beechmast, and acorns. They also readily eat mushrooms."

45 Psalm 119: "Blessed are the undefiled in the way, who walk in the law of the Lord. Blessed are they that keep his testimonies, and that seek him with the whole heart. They also do no iniquity: they walk in his ways. Thou hast commanded us to keep thy precepts diligently. O that my ways were directed to keep thy statutes! Then shall I not be ashamed, when I have respect unto all they commandments. I will praise thee with uprightness of heart, when I shall have learned thy righteous judgements. I will keep thy statutes: O forsake me not utterly. . . . Thy word have I hid in mine heart. . . . I have gone astray like a lost sheep; seek thy servant; for I do not forget thy commandments." Please read this entire Psalm to truly understand the importance of learning and following and keeping the Lord's commandments.

2 Timothy 3:14–17: "But continue thou in the things which thou hast learned and hast been assured of, knowing of whom thou hast learned them; and that from a child thou hast known the holy scriptures, which are able to make thee wise unto salvation through faith which is in Christ Jesus. All Scripture is given by inspiration of God, and is profitable for doctrine, for reproof, for correction, for instruction in righteousness: that the man of God may be perfect, thoroughly furnished unto all good works."

2 Peter 1:19–21: We have also a more sure word of proph-

CREATIONWISE

THE BIBLE IS *100%* TRUTH, FROM START TO FINISH!

LATER THE BIBLE HAS SOME MYTHS, BUT IS MOSTLY TRUE!

LATER THE BIBLE HAS LOTS OF MYTHS AND SOME TRUTH.

LATER HOGWASH!

SAD BUT TRUE – THIS KIND OF EVOLUTION DOES HAPPEN!

esy; whereunto ye do well that ye take heed, as unto a light that shineth in a dark place, until the day dawn, and the day star arise in your hearts: knowing this first, that no prophecy of the scripture is of any private interpretation. For the prophesy came not in old time by the will of man: but holy men of God spake as they were moved by the Holy Ghost."

46 Some have argued that people or animals would have been hurt even in an "ideal" world. They contend that even before sin Adam could have stood on small creatures, or scratched himself on a branch and so on. They say that animals could have easily hurt themselves walking over rocks — bumping into things, etc. Now these sorts of situations are true of today's FALLEN world — but the point is, the present world is NOT perfect — it is suffering from the effects of the curse (Rom. 8:22). One can't look at the Bible through the world's "eyes" and insist that the world before sin was just like the world we see today. We do not know what a perfect world, continually restored and upheld 100 percent by God's power (Col. 1:17; Heb. 1:3) would be like — we have never experienced perfection (only Adam and Eve did before sin). But, we do get a little glimpse from Scripture: For instance, in Deuteronomy 8:4; 29:5 and Nehemiah 9:21, we are told that when the Israelites wandered in the desert for 40 years, their clothes and shoes did not wear out, nor did their feet swell. This is the opposite of what happens to us in the present world — however, when God

upholds things perfect — wearing out or being harmed or hurt in any way is not even an option. Also, think of Shadrach, Meshach, and Abednego (Dan. 3:26–27) —

Dilophosaurus

they went into the fire and came out without even the smell of fire on them. Again — when the Lord upholds perfectly — being hurt is NOT possible. In a perfect world, before sin and the curse, God would have upheld EVERYTHING like these examples — but in this cursed world, things now wear out and run down. Also read Isaiah 11:6–9. Many commentators believe this description of the wolf and lamb and lion who eats straw like an ox, to be a picture of what the new earth will be like in the future restoration (Acts 3:21) when there will be no more curse or death (Rev. 21:1; 22:3). The description here is one of animals that would normally attack others living peacefully together as vegetarians (this is also the description of the animal world before sin — Gen. 1:30). The point is, the world we live in has been changed dramatically because of sin and the curse. The present food chain and behavior of animals (which was changed after the flood in Gen. 9:2–3) CANNOT be used as a basis for interpreting the Bible — the Bible explains WHY the world is the way it is!

47 Morris, *The Genesis Record*, p. 78.
48 Richard Leakey and Roger Lewin, *The Sixth Extinction: Patterns of Life and the Future of Humankind* (New York: Doubleday, 1995), p. 44. "Earth history evidently is not

one of gradualistic progression, as Lyell and Darwin fervently desired, but one of sporadic and spasmodic convulsions." p. 59. "The history of life on earth is punctuated by occasional bursts of extinction, some moderate, some catastrophic; of that there is no doubt."

49 Genesis 7:2–3 "Of every clean beast thou shalt take to thee by sevens, the male and his female: and of beasts that are not clean by two, the male and his female. Of fowls also of the air by sevens, the male and the female; to keep seed alive upon the face of the earth."

Michael Kruger, personal communication. "An Understanding of Genesis 7:2. The question before us is: 'If the natural reading of Genesis 7:2 ('of every clean beast thou shalt take to thee by sevens, the male and his female') is understood to mean seven pairs or fourteen individuals; would not the natural reading of the rest of that verse ('of the beasts that are not clean by two, the male and his female') be understood to mean two pairs or four individuals?' This question has been raised by many commentators and there are various suggestions concerning how to understand this verse. I will offer what I think is the best solution. First, when we look at 7:2 in the King James text we see a parallel between 'by sevens' and 'by two' and thus it only seems natural that they should be understood in the same manner. However, when the Hebrew text is examined we see that the parallelism breaks down. The phrase 'by sevens' is literally rendered 'seven seven' (שׁבעה שׁבעה) because the Hebrew word for the number seven occurs twice. In contrast, the following phrase 'by two' does not have the word 'two' (שׁעם) twice, but it only appears once in the Hebrew text. Thus, the latter phrase in the King James text 'by two' could better be rendered simply 'two.' . . . Now that we have established that only two of every unclean animal went onto the ark, we now can turn our attention to understanding the number of clean animals that went onto the ark by examining this peculiar phrase 'seven seven'; or as the King James puts it 'by sevens.' This method of writing the number twice is very common in Hebrew literature and even appears later in chapter seven in v. 9 and 15. In these verses we see the phrase 'two by two' used which can literally be rendered 'two two.' When two numbers are placed beside each other such as in 7:9, 15 and also in 7:2 (seven seven) it is what is called the 'distributive' use of numbers (see Paul Jouon, *A Grammar of Biblical Hebrew*, 142 p; p.530.) This simply means that the phrase 'seven seven' can be understood as 'seven each.' In other words, God was commanding Noah to take seven of each clean animal and two of each unclean animal. The fact that 'two two' (7:9, 15) simply means 'two each' is confirmed by 7:2 where we are clearly told that only two of each unclean was to be taken on the ark. If 'two two' certainly means only two individuals, then why wouldn't 'seven seven' also mean seven individuals? There is no need to postulate seven pairs or fourteen individuals. The only reason that interpretation of seven individuals is resisted is because it is an odd number that makes one ask, 'Why seven?' We now turn to that very question. If 'seven seven' means only seven individuals then we have three pairs of male and female and then one male left over. What is the purpose of this extra clean male animal? Genesis 8:20 gives us the answer: 'And Noah builded an altar unto the Lord; and took of every clean beast, and of every clean fowl, and offered burnt offerings on the altar.' The obvious explanation of seven animals is so that one could be offered as a sacrifice to the Lord after they got off the ark. Henry Morris agrees with this interpretation, 'The three pairs (of clean animals) were to encourage the relatively greater numerical proliferation of the clean animals after the flood . . . the seventh animal in each group was clearly intended for sacrificial

purposes' (Morris, *The Genesis Record*, p.191)."
50 Michael Crichton, *The Lost World* (New York: Ballantine
Books, 1995), p. 122. "Dinosaurs were mostly small. . . .
People always think they were huge, but the average dinosaur was the size of a sheep, or a small pony."
Horner and Lessem, *The Complete T. rex*, p. 124. "It's not
size. *T. rex* was horribly big, but most dinosaurs were
smaller than bulls."
51 Lambert, *A Field Guide to Dinosaurs*, p. 127.
"*Hypselosaurus* probably laid big eggs like this — actual size 1 ft. (30 cm) long by 10 in. (25 cm) across, with
a 5.8 pint (3.3 liter) capacity. Probably no dinosaur laid
eggs any larger."
Lucas, *Dinosaurs — The Textbook*, p. 193. "The largest
dinosaur eggs, those of sauropods, were more than 30
cm long."
52 Lessem and Glut, *The Dinosaur Society's Dinosaur Encyclopedia*, p. xiv. "This book is an alphabetical, illustrated
catalogue of all the dinosaur genera and many of the
species that have ever been formally named. These totals are now
calculated at
446 genera,
113 of which
are of doubt-
ful validity,
and 665 spe-
cies, 213 of
which are of
doubtful va-
lidity. These
totals do not

Protoceratops

include synonyms, many of which are also listed here.
So many popular dinosaur books call dinosaurs only by
their first, or generic, names that we forget that several,
quite different, species may sometimes be included in

any one genus. Which big cat would we exhibit for the genus *Panthera*, the tiger (*Panthera tigris*), the lion (*Panthera leo*), or the leopard (*Panthera pardus*)? Likewise, by focusing on the individual species rather than just the genera, we obtain a more realistic picture of dinosaurian diversity."

53 Lane P. Lester and Raymond G. Bohlin, *The Natural Limits to Biological Change* (Dallas, TX: Probe Books, 1989), p. 156–169. This section discusses the difference between a species and a kind and attempts to present the limits and boundaries of a created kind.

Frank L. Marsh, *Variation and Fixity in Nature* (Mountain View, CA: Pacific Press Publ. Assoc., 1976), p. 87–91. This section discusses the difference between a species and a kind and also shows that God created limits and fixity into His created kinds so that a dog will always produce a dog and a cat a cat.

Gary Parker, *Creation: Facts of Life* (Green Forest, AR: Master Books, 1994), p. 115–122. Discusses how evolutionists use speciation to define evolution, but it is nothing more than the variation within a kind. For when two species of flies no longer interbreed, that is not proof of evolution by the forming of new species, but is actually a loss of genetic information within two members of a created kind.

Kurt P. Wise, "Practical Baraminology," *Creation ex nihilo Technical Journal,* Vol. 6(2), 1992, p. 122–137. This article discusses the new field of baraminology or the classification of created kinds.

John Woodmorappe, *Noah's Ark: A Feasibility Study* (El Cajon, CA: Institute for Creation Research, 1996), p. 6–7. "Jones (1972b), largely using scriptural evidence (e.g., the animal lists in Leviticus), demonstrated that the created kind is approximately equivalent to the subfamily or family level, at least in the case of birds and mammals. Recently, Scherer (1993) has arrived at the same conclusion, but on the basis of scientific evidence. This evidence includes numerous documented cases of inter-breeding between individuals of different species and genera, as well as interbreeding with a third species or genus in situations where two species or genera do not themselves interbreed."

54 Bill Mehlert, "On the Origin of Cats and Carnivores," *Creation ex nihilo Technical Journal*, Vol. 9(1), 1995, p. 106–120. This article discusses the differences between evolutionary species and the biblical kind as found in the opening part of the Abstract: "Creation scientists are working on ways to identify the biblical 'kinds'; the created units or groups as described in the Book of Genesis." The article then proceeds to examine the "cat family" from a created kind perspective and concludes with this statement: "On the basis of the available evidence (and lack of it), therefore, it is my conclusion that a process which Richard Carrington once described as a 'series of accidents' could hardly produce the amazing complexity and variability we see in the cats and other carnivores, or for that matter in all the rest of the organic world. The evidence taken as a whole seems to point in the direction of a creator/designer and away from a chance natural process. It is therefore my belief that the cat barmin (or at most two of these, with many common design features) was created by God with the inbuilt genetic capabilities of diversifying in order to meet the demands of the varying environments encountered since creation."

55 Parker, *Creation: Facts of Life*, p. 104. "To make evolution happen — or even to make evolution a scientific theory — evolutionists need some kind of 'genetic script writer' to increase the quantity and quality of genetic information. Mutations are just 'typographic errors' that occur as genetic script is copied. Mutations have no ability to compose genetic sentences, and thus no ability to make evolution happen at all." p. 117. "Any

real evolution (macroevolution) requires an expansion of the gene pool, the addition of new genes and new traits as life is supposed to move from simple beginnings to ever more varied and complex forms ('molecules to man' or 'fish to philosopher'). Suppose there are islands where

Heterodontosaurus

varieties of flies that used to trade genes no longer interbreed. Is this evidence for evolution? No, exactly the opposite. Each variety resulting from reproductive isolation has a smaller gene pool than the original and a restricted ability to explore new environments with new trait combinations or to meet changes in its own environment. The long-term result? Extinction would be much more likely than evolution."

Carl Wieland, *Stones and Bones* (Acacia Ridge, Queensland, Australia: Creation Science Foundation, Ltd.; 1994), p. 18–20. "So to go from A to B in the diagram would require many steps, each involving an INCREASE IN INFORMATION. Information coding from new structures, new functions — new, useful complexity. If we saw those sorts of information-increasing changes happening, even if only a few, this could reasonably be used to help support the argument that fish may, indeed, change into philosophers, given enough time. In fact, however, the many small changes we do see do not involve increasing information — they are heading in the wrong direction to be used in support of evolution."

56 Lambert, *A Field Guide to Dinosaurs*, p. 92. "More than a dozen kinds of flesh-eating dinosaurs are known only

from teeth or pieces of bone that are so few or so broken that we cannot say what family they came from. Some may not belong to dinosaurs." p. 100. "One scientist thinks that they were just the young of the bigger, broader-footed plateosaurids." p. 103. "*Euskelosaurus* ('well-limbed lizard') may be the same kind as most others often called melanorosaurids." p. 134. "A few sauropods fit no family so far described. Others are known only from puzzling fragments." p. 134. "*Clasmodosaurus* ('fragment tooth lizard') is known only from teeth once thought to have come from a flesh-eating dinosaur." p. 162. "*Orthomerus* ('having straight parts') is known from straight leg bones found in the Netherlands and southern Russia. *Orthomerus* may be the same as *Telmatosaurus*." p. 163. "*Tanius* ('of the Tan'). This Chinese hadrosaurid was probably like Edmontosaurus but most of the front of its head remains unknown." (From page 161) *Edmontosaurus* ('Edmonton lizard') from Alberta, Montana, and New Jersey."

57 Woodmorappe, *Noah's Ark: A Feasibility Study*, p. 13. "Mass Distribution of the Animals on the Ark. As can be seen from the census (Tables 1 and 2), the vast majority of the animals on the ark were small. Without allowing the representation of large animals as juveniles, the median animal on the ark would have been the size of a small rat (about 100 grams)."

58 John C. Whitcomb and Henry M. Morris, *The Genesis Flood* (Phillipsburg, NJ: Presbyterian and Reformed Pub. Co., 1961), p. 65–69. "For all practical purposes, one could say that, at the outside, there was need for no more than 35,000 individual vertebrate animals on the ark. The total number of so-called species of mammals, birds, reptiles, and amphibians listed by Mayr is 17,600, but undoubtedly the number of original 'kinds' was less than this. Assuming the average size of these animals to be about that of a sheep (there are only a very few really

large animals, of course, and even these could have been represented on the ark by young ones), the following will give an idea of the accommodations available: The number of animals per car [railroad stock cars] varies greatly, depending on the size and age of the animals . . . reports of stock cars and railroads show that the average number of meat animals to the carload is for cattle about 25, hogs in single deck cars about 75, and sheep about 120 per deck. This means that at least 240 animals of the size of sheep could be accommodated in a standard two-decked stock car. Two trains hauling 73 such cars each would thus be ample to carry the 35,000 animals. We have already seen that the ark had a carrying capacity equivalent to that of 522 stock cars of this size! We therefore find that a few simple calculations dispose of this trivial objection once and for all."

Woodmorappe, *Noah's Ark: A Feasibility Study*, p. 3–16. p. 3 — "Did the ark actually have to carry every type of animal in existence? Modern anti-creationists continue to resurrect long-discredited tomfooleries about the overcrowded ark. For instance, although it was shown long ago that the ark was not required to carry every member of Kingdom Animalia, recent critics continue to burlesque the ark by placing just about every imaginable living thing on it. Morton has visions of snails and earthworms struggling for thousands of years to make it to the ark in time. Moore fantasizes that the ark carried deep-sea fish. McGown, not to be outdone, puts whales and sharks on the ark. Futuyma adds to the farce by repositing all the millions of plant and animal species onto the ark. Schneour and Plimer take rationalistic arguments against the ark to new heights of absurdity by insisting that it had to carry cultures of microorganisms! At the other extreme, we have compromising evangelicals (e.g., Hugh Ross, 1990) who want to "save" the flood by insisting that Noah only had to carry a few common domesticated

CREATIONWISE

LOOK AT THAT BEAUTIFUL RAINBOW! IT'S A PROMISE FROM GOD THAT HE'LL NEVER*AGAIN FLOOD THE ENTIRE EARTH AS HE DID IN NOAH'S DAY!

MY CHRISTIAN COLLEGE PROFESSOR SAID THAT NOAH'S FLOOD DIDN'T COVER THE ENTIRE EARTH.
*GENESIS 9:8-17

HE TOLD YOU IT WAS JUST A "LOCALIZED" FLOOD?

THAT'S WHAT HE SAID!

SO HE BELIEVES THAT GOD PROMISED TO NEVER AGAIN SEND A "LOCALIZED" FLOOD?

DAN LIETHA

animals on the ark. Needless to say, Scripture does not limit the contents of the ark to domesticated animals. Neither, for that matter, does Jewish tradition." p. 16 — "We can see from Table 3 that less that half the cumulative area of the ark's three decks need to have been occupied by the animals and their enclosures. Furthermore, this assumes no tiering of the enclosures, which of course maximizes the ark floor space needed for animal housing, but also allows at least some of the food and water to be stored overhead. There is plenty of room left over to account for the ark infrastructure, and passageways between the animal enclosures, although the latter need not consume much additional floor area.

59 Roy D. Holt, "Evidence for a Late Cainozoic Flood/post-Flood Boundary," *Creation ex nihilo Technical Journal*, Vol. 10(1), 1996, p. 128–167. In discussing the evidences for a flood/post-flood geologic boundary, Holt consistently refers to the Ice Age as occurring some time after the flood and having a great deal of affect on many areas including fluctuations in the ocean levels which in themselves would have had drastic affects with changes as great as 40 meters.

Michael J. Oard, *An Ice Age Caused by the Genesis Flood* (El Cajon, CA: Institute for Creation Research, 1990). This technical monograph explores the many different theories that have been proposed as the mechanisms by which an Ice Age could have occurred and all of which have serious deficiencies except one, as a result of the flood of Genesis. Oard gives strong evidence to show that the after-effects of the Genesis flood would have been sufficient to have caused an Ice Age. In his concluding remarks, he says on page 187: "The proposed mechanism is catastrophic, and is not based on the uniformitarian principle. Specifically, the Ice Age is treated as a consequence of the Genesis flood, which disrupted the climate to such a degree that an Ice Age developed immediately afterwards."

60 Mace Baker, *DINOSAURS* (Redding, CA: New Century Books, 1991), p. 156. In discussion of Dinosaur National Monument: "Approximately 20 complete skeletons were extracted from this uplifted matrix as well as bones and parts of skeletons representing nearly 300 individual dinosaurs. By 1972, 700,000 pounds of dinosaur material had been transported to the Carnegie Museum. In this one compact treasury of fossils, thirteen separate dinosaur species were identified. It is interesting to note that this area is regarded as once having been a low, tropic land. Here we see rather idyllic conditions for the perpetuation of the reptilian species. It is highly improbable that such a concentration can represent a series of natural deaths. This fossil graveyard points very deliberately to an overwhelming catastrophe which killed and buried a large number of dinosaurs living in the same general area."

Czerkas and Czerkas. *Dinosaurs: A Global View*, p. 151. "The Dinosaur National Monument is unique in having a broad representation of almost all of the different types of dinosaurs that are known to have lived during the Late Jurassic. Within a coarse conglomerate of pebbles and stones are the entangled remains of many of the best-known dinosaurs. The remains of *Allosaurus* and *Stegosaurus*, and sauropods including *Barosaurus*, *Diplodocus* and *Apatosaurus* (which is best known by its popular, though incorrect name *Brontosaurus*) have been revealed on an uplifted wall of stone. The surrounding matrix, being made up of small coarse stones, reveals that the bodies of these dinosaurs were carried along a powerful and fast-moving river and eventually came to rest on the bank along the bend of channels that quickly entombed them to form a shrine within the earth. Successive layers show that periodic catastrophes plagued these dinosaurs preserving their remains through the vast expanse of time to be revealed once again in a monument to their existence."

Norell et.al., *Discovering Dinosaurs in the American Museum of Natural History*, p. 86–87. Page 86 shows a photograph of the Howe Quarry, Wyoming, with the following caption on the next page: "FIGURE 56. The Museum's most prolific dinosaur collector was Barnum Brown, who organized the excavation of the Howe Quarry in the Jurassic Morrison Formation of Wyoming. This quarry contained hundreds of disarticulated sauropod bones, as well as the partial skeleton of a juvenile *Diplodocus* (or possibly *Barosaurus*) that is now on exhibit in the Roosevelt Memorial Hall."

The Weekend Australian, Nov. 26–27, 1983, p. 32. For example, reptiles drowned in a flash flood 200 million years ago, according to the interpretation put upon the discovery of reptile fossils in the Lubnock Quarry, Texas.

Linda West and Dan Chure, *Dinosaur: The Dinosaur National Monument Quarry* (Jensen, UT: Dinosaur Nature Assoc., 1989), p. 4. "Already preserved from decay by fairly rapid burial in river sands and gravels which hardened into a tough sandstone, the bones that Douglas would later discover were now well-protected by this mile-thick covering."

61 *NIV Study Bible* (Grand Rapids, MI: Zondervan Bible Publishers, 1985), p. 778. Job 40:15 — footnote v — "Possibly the hippopotamus or elephant."

62 *New Living Translation — Holy Bible* (Wheaton, IL:

Tyndale House Publishers, 1996), p. 562. Job 40:15 —
"Take a look at the mighty hippopotamus."

63 Boughton Cobb, *A Field Guide to the Ferns* (Boston, MA:
Houghton Mifflin Co., 1963), p. 254–255.

64 Carl Wieland, " 'Lost World' Animals Found!" *Creation
ex nihilo,* Vol. 19(1), 1996, p. 10–13. "Tantalizing rumors of huge, unusual elephants, with features similar
to extinct elephant types like the mammoth, have circu-
lated for years in remote areas of western Nepal. . . . His

[Colonel John Blashford-Snell] discovery of two of these elephants has confirmed the rumors and sent a buzz through the scientific community. . . . Their features happen to be remarkably like those shown in cave drawings of the mammoths, for example in southwest France, which are dated by evolutionists to as much as 30,000 years (and never less than 10,000 years) ago. These distinctive characteristics include unusually sloping backs, 'reptilian' appearance to the tail, a swept-up forehead and a large dome-shaped hump on the top of their heads."

65 Anon., "Sensational Australia Tree . . . Like 'Finding a Live Dinosaur,' " *Creation ex nihilo,* Vol. 17(2), 1995, p. 13. "Professor Carrick Chambers, Director of the Royal Botanic Gardens in Sydney, has said of the sensational discovery of a type of tree in Australia's Blue Mountains (200 kilometers west of Sydney, in Wollemi National Park) that it was like finding a 'live dinosaur.' This is because the tree, nicknamed the Wollemi pine, is known from fossils classed as so-called Jurassic age around 150 million years ago, but not from fossils in rocks of later periods."

66 *Melbourne Sun*, Feb. 6, 1980. More than 40 people claimed to have seen plesiosaurs off the Victorian coast (Australia) over recent years.

67 Anon., "Dinosaur Hunt," *Science Digest*, Vol. 89, No. 5., June 1981, p. 21. Herman A. Regusters, "Mokele-Mbembe: An Investigation into Rumors Concerning A Strange Animal in the Republic of the Congo, *Munger Afrinana Library Notes,* Issue 64, July 1981, p. 2–32.
    Science Frontiers, No. 33, 1983. Refers to: Marcelin Agmagna, "Results of the First Congolese Mokele-Mbembe Expedition," *Cryptozoology*, Vol. 2, 1983, p. 103.

68 Dennis L. Swift, "Messages on Stone," *Creation ex nihilo*, Vol. 19(2), 1997, p. 20-23. "Did ancient man leave mute testimonies on libraries of stone that he lived with

dinosaurs and other animals considered long extinct? Scientific evidence is amassing of such 'prehistoric' creatures depicted on caves, rock formations and other artifacts. These may be either as pictographs (picture symbols) or petroglyphs (carved rock drawings). . . . Fran Barnes, a recognized authority on rock art of the American South-West, writes, 'In the San Rafael Swell, there is a pictograph that looks very much like a pterosaur, a Cretaceous flying reptile.' . . . Photo 5 shows a petroglyph in Arizona's Havasupai Canyon of a creature with the unmistakable upright stance and balancing tail of some of the known dinosaurs, but unlike any other creature. Barnes writes, 'There is a petroglyph in Natural Bridges National Monument that bears a startling resemblance to a dinosaur, specifically a *Brontosaurus*, with a long tail and neck, small head and all.' Note that Barnes, who despises creationists, knows that this work shows every sign of age, such as pitting and weathering, etc. If there was an 'orthodox' way to explain these sorts of finds away, he would have tried to do so."

69 Joachim Scheven, *Living Fossils: Confirmation of Creation* (Queensland, Australia: Creation Videos, Creation Science Foundation, 1992)."While it's commonly known that many of the fossil creatures are no longer with us, even most scientists are unaware that there are literally hundreds of examples alive today, which are also found as fossils, unchanged, even though they're allegedly separated by millions of years. The evidence of these so-called living fossils strongly supports the biblical account that fossils are young and that basic kinds do not change."

Triceratops skull

70 Currie and Padian, editors, *The Encyclopedia of Dinosaurs,* "Jurassic Park," by Schweitzer and Lessem, p. 386–387. "Currently, we can 'clone' an organism in one of two ways. First, we can induce a fertilized egg to split and then develop independently as two individuals. This process is similar to that which gives rise to identical twins. Alternatively, we can remove a fertilized nucleus from one cell and insert it into an anucleate cell from a similar or identical organism and then place this cell into the proper environment for development. This latter method would have to be used with our dinosaur genetic material. However, with dinosaurs, we have no cells in which to insert our manufactured blueprint. It is not just the DNA that is crucial to correct development. Hormonal and environmental cues act upon the developing cells in order to provide signals for the production of developmental proteins and physiological changes. Sometimes this environment is strongly temperature dependent, but we do not know the temperature at which dinosaurs incubated their Eggs. Again, we would only have living relatives as a guide, and maybe this educated guesswork would be sufficient for some dinosaur taxa, but certainly not all of them. However, suppose that all these problems could be overcome. Suppose that we could find enough DNA to ensure that it was really dinosaurian; that we could piece together the vast majority of DNA that was missing or degraded or damaged from pieces of bird or crocodile DNA; that we could learn how many chromosomes a *Tyrannosaur*, a *Triceratops*, an *Apatosaurus*, or a *Gallimimus* possessed; that we could correctly guess the placement of every single base pair with the correct number of intervening noncoding sequences, on each chromosome; that we could find the appropriate "host" cell to receive this genetic cocktail; and that we could find the right combination of temperatures, light, hormones, and other protein signals to ensure proper

development, to the point that we could produce a living dinosaur embryo. The odds against this occurring are astronomical, but even if it did, we would still be a very long way from Jurassic Park (or, more accurately, Cretaceous Park). The dinosaur's genetic programming would be designed to deal with the environment, the foods, the enzymes, the diseases, and the parasites of the world as it was at least 65 million years ago. If it was a plant eater, the enzymes produced in its digestive tract would be designed to break down plants with which it had co-evolved. Sixty-five million years of changes in plant proteins, cell walls, and toxins would have occurred in the plants descended from those on which the dinosaur fed. Most of the plants that made up its Diet are long extinct."

Carl Wieland. Letter written March 25, 1997, on the cloning of Dolly the sheep. "The egg which was used for the fertilization did NOT contribute any DNA. It had its nucleus removed, so it had no nuclear DNA to contribute. However, there are factors in the cytoplasm of the mammalian egg which are needed for the expression of the information in the nucleus of the fertilized cell."

71 Norell et.al., *Discovering Dinosaurs in the American Museum of Natural History*, p. 13. "The contemporary perspective on the origin of birds began to develop in the mid-1960s. About this time John Ostrom, a paleontologist at Yale University, made the first in a series of important discoveries improving our understanding of bird origins."

72 Virginia Morell, "Origin of Birds: The Dinosaur Debate."
Audubon, March/April 1997, p. 38.

73 Anon., "New 'Birdosaur' NOT Missing Link!" Creation
ex nihilo, Vol. 15(3), 1993, p. 3. "A RECENT issue of
Time magazine has a special feature on dinosaurs. On
the cover, readers are told there is a 'new link between
dinosaurs and birds.' Discovered in the Gobi desert of
Mongolia, the turkey-sized *Mononychus* ('one claw') is
shown on the front cover looking like a half-bird, half-
dinosaur. It is covered with fine feathers and has a long
feathery tail. . . . What about the feathers shown on the
cover? We learn on page 52 that the feathers are sur-
mised by an evolutionary chain of reasoning, not having
been apparent on the fossil specimen — it was 'probably covered with feathers.' *Time* (Australia), April 26,
1993. It is sad to consider that many may be misled by
seeing a beautifully illustrated creature with feathers
billed as a 'link' on the cover of this high-circulation
magazine, especially as the feathers are, so far, imagi-
nary."

Anon., " 'Birdosaur' More Like a Mole," *Creation ex
nihilo*, Vol. 15(4), 1993, p. 7. "A NEW dinosaur called
Mononychus, which we mentioned last issue, had some
bird-like features (keeled sternum and bird-like wrists,
among others), so it was called a 'link' between dinosaurs and birds. It was shown with feathers on a recent
cover of *Time* magazine, even though it was definitely
non-flying, had lived (by evolutionary reasoning) a long
time after its alleged flying ancestor, and no feathers had
been found. Now a reassessment of its short, stubby,
single-clawed forelimbs suggests that they were most
likely used for digging. The author of the article states
that 'moles and other diggers have keeled sternums and
wrists reminiscent of birds.' *Science News*, Vol. 143, No.
16, April 17, 1993 (p. 245). We wonder — will there be
a front-page retraction from *Time* in due course? Their

spectacular drawing has been seen by millions, further cementing belief that there really are such things as definite evolutionary transitions."

74 The following list is just some of the newspaper reports that were received by the Answers in Genesis information department concerning the so-called feathered dinosaur from China:

"Downy Dinosaur Reported — Scientists see early ancestor to birds," *Cincinnati Enquirer*, Oct. 19, 1996, p. A13.

"Find may link birds, dinosaurs. A fossil dinosaur found in China displays evidence of feathery down, the first discovery of its kind." *Colorado Dispatch*, Oct. 20, 1996.

"Chinese fossil find links dinosaurs and birds." *The Herald*, Oct. 18, 1996.

"Feathery fossil hints dinosaur, bird link." *Pacific Stars and Stripes*, Oct. 22, 1996.

"Fossil beefs up theory dinos-aves birds of a feather," *Jackson Hole Daily, Weekend*, Oct. 18-20, 1996.

"Dinosaur fossil is in fine feather." *Seattle Post Intelligence*, Oct. 19, 1996.

"Feathery Fossil Suggests Birds Are Descended From Dinosaurs." *San Francisco Chronicle*, Oct. 18, 1996.

"Feathered fossil firms dinosaur-bird bridge." *The Daily Gazette,* Schenectady, N.Y., Oct. 18, 1996.

"Feathered fossil may show that dinosaurs sprouted wings." *The Huntsville Times*, Oct. 18, 1996.

"Fossil find suggests dinosaur-bird link." *Lincoln Journal Star*, Oct. 20, 1996.

75 "Chinese fossil find links dinosaurs and birds." *The Herald*, Oct. 18, 1996. (Associated Press article out of New York). "Photographs of the fossilized creature show an unmistakable downy stripe running down its back. If the feathered dinosaur is confirmed, then it provides almost irrefutable evidence that today's birds evolved from dinosaurs."

76 "Chinese fossil find links dinosaurs and birds." *The Her-*

ald, Oct. 18, 1996. (Associated Press article out of New York). "'As soon as they showed me the specimen it just blew me away,' said Phil Currie, a paleontologist who recently saw the fossil in Beijing. 'You can't come to any conclusion other than that they're feathers.' "

77 Bill Stieg, "Did Birds Evolve From Dinosaurs?" *The Philadelphia Inquirer,* March 1997. "A 'dream team' of American scientists traveled to China to check out an amazing report: A dinosaur fossil that seemed to have feathers. In the National Geological Museum in Beijing, Director Ji Qiang assists visitors John Ostrom, Alan Brush, Larry D. Martin, and Peter Wellnhofer as they huddle over fossils from a northeastern China site."

78 Stieg, "Did Birds Evolve From Dinosaurs?" " 'I'm just not convinced,' agreed the ornithologist Brush. He pulled on a Yankees cap as he took a break from the microscope and sat in the Beijing museum's quiet courtyard. He said he saw 'hair-like' structures — not hairs — that could have supported a frill, or crest, like those on iguanas. 'On reptiles there are many kind of structures that would be like this,' he said. 'On birds there are structures, like eyelashes and bristles around the mouth, that could be like this.' The scientists don't know how the structures formed, or what they were made of — just that they probably weren't feathers."

79 Paul Recer, "Birds Linked to Dinosaurs," *Cincinnati Enquirer*, May, 21, 1997, p. A9. "... fossils with winglike forearms suggest a Patagonian lizard shared a common

CREATIONWISE

CREATION QUIZ!
WHICH OF THE FOLLOWING CREATURES HAVE BEEN ON EARTH THE LONGEST?

ANSWERS:
A, C, & D HAVE BEEN AROUND THE LONGEST! ALL CREATED ON DAY 5. (GEN. 1:20-23)
ALL LAND ANIMALS (INCLUDING DINOS) WERE CREATED ON DAY 6!! (GEN. 1:24-31)
BELIEVE IT!

dinosaur ancestor with modern birds. Fresh support for the birds-from-dinosaurs theory comes just as Hollywood unleashes more toothy Jurassic terrors. Twenty fossil bones uncovered in an ancient riverbed in Argentina are from a 90-million-year-old flightless animal with shoulders and forearms that could flap up and down like wings, an Argentina paleontologist announced Tuesday. Fernando Novas of the Museum of Natural History in Buenos Aires, Argentina, said the bones are from the 'most bird-like dinosaur ever recovered' and gives powerful new evidence that the gentle world of birds evolved millions of years ago from the 'terrible lizards.' "

80 Stieg, "Did Birds Evolve From Dinosaurs?" "Martin didn't see anything to change his opinion that this was no warm-blooded bird relative. Recent research has shown the microscopic structure of dinosaur bones was 'characteristic of cold-blooded animals,' Martin said. 'So we're back to cold-blooded dinosaurs.' "

81 Recer, "Birds Linked to Dinosaurs," "Though they bear little resemblance to relentless killers depicted in *The Lost World: Jurassic Park,* he said, 'Parrots and hummingbirds are also dinosaurs.' "

Norell et.al., *Discovering Dinosaurs in the American Museum of Natural History*, p. 25. "Figure 19. The smallest dinosaur is the bee hummingbird, *Mellisuga helenae*, found only in Cuba. The male of this diminutive bird reaches an adult weight of only 1.95 grams."

82 Ann C. Burke and Alan Feduccia, "Developmental Patterns and the Identification of Homologies in the Avian Hand," *Science*, Vol. 278, Oct. 24, 1997, p. 666–668. "Homologies of digits in the avian hand have been debated for 150 years. Cladistic analysis nests birds with theropod dinosaurs. Theropod hands retain only digits I-II-III, so digits of the modern bird hand are often identified as I-II-III. Study of the developing manus and pes in amniote embryos, including a variety of avian spe-

cies, shows stereotyped patterns of cartilage condensations. A primary axis of cartilage condensation is visible in all species that runs through the humerus into digit IV. Comparison to serially homologous elements of the hindlimb indicates that the retain digits of the avian hand are II-III-IV."

83 John A. Ruben, Terry D. Jones, Nicholas R. Geist, and W. Jaap Hillenius, "Lung Structure and Ventilation in Theropod Dinosaurs and Early Birds," *Science*, Vol. 278, Nov. 14, 1997, p. 1267–1270. "Reptiles and birds possess separate lungs rather than the alveolar-style lungs of mammals. The morphology of the unmodified, bellows-like septate lung restricts the maximum rates of respiratory gas exchange. Among taxa possessing septate lungs, only the modified avian flow-through lung is capable of the oxygen-carbon dioxide exchange rates that are typical of active endotherms. Paleontological and neontological evidence indicates that theropod dinosaurs possessed unmodified, bellows-like septate lungs that were ventilated with a crocodile-like hepatic-piston diaphragm. The earliest birds (*Archaeopteryx* and enantiornithines) also possessed unmodified septate lungs but lacked a hepatic-piston diaphragm mechanism. These data are consistent with an ectothermic status for theropod dinosaurs and early birds."

84 Ann Gibbons, "Plucking the Feathered Dinosaur," *Science*, Vol. 278, Nov. 14, 1997, p. 1229.

85 Theistic evolutionists basically accept the teachings of popular evolutionary theory (and the millions of years history for the fossil record), but say that God used evolution to "create."

86 Progressive creationists do not accept popular evolutionary theory per se — but they do accept much of what current evolutionists teach in astronomy and biology (particularly the millions of years history of the fossil record). This position holds that God continually created species

of creatures and plants of millions of years as they kept going extinct. Most who hold this position would claim that Noah's flood was only a local event.

87 There are many different variations of the gap theory — but the main version, sometimes called the "ruin-reconstruction" theory, accepts millions of years for the age of the fossil record, but has all these events occurring in a gap between Genesis 1:1 and Genesis 1:2. For a detailed refutation of the gap theory, see *Unformed and Unfilled*, by Weston Fields (Collinsville, IL: Burgeners Enterprises, 1976).

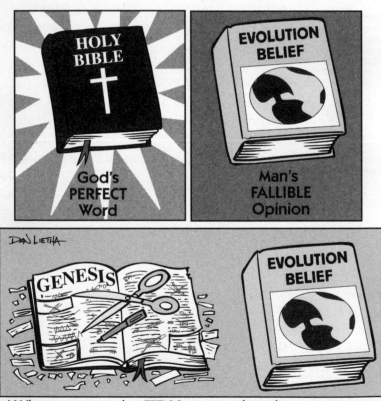

When people **TRY** to make them agree, guess which one gets **"MODIFIED"**!!!!

APPENDIX B
REFERENCES

The following references for the information given about each of the major illustrations in this book provide a wonderful source of material for those wishing to further research the exciting topic of dinosaurs. These publications should be readily available from any major library.

Tyrannosaurus Rex
Philip J. Currie and Kevin Padian, editors, *Encyclopedia of Dinosaurs*, "Size and Scaling," by R. McNeill Alexander (San Diego, CA: Academic Press, 1997), p. 665–667.

Philip J. Currie and Kevin Padian, editors, *Encyclopedia of Dinosaurs*, "Tyrannosauridae," by Kenneth Carpenter (San Diego, CA: Academic Press, 1997), p. 665–667.

Dougal Dixon, Barry Cox, R.J.G. Savage, and Brian Gardiner, *The MacMillan Illustrated Encyclopedia of Dinosaurs and Prehistoric Animals* (New York: Macmillan Publishing Co., 1988), p. 121.

Tim Gardom and Angela Milner, *The Book of Dinosaurs: The Natural History Museum Guide* (Rocklin, CA: Prima Publishing, 1993), p. 123.

John R. Horner and Don Lessem, *The Complete T. rex* (New York: Simon & Schuster, 1993), p. 17–77.

Larry McShane, "T-Rex Sue sells for $8.4M," *Cincinnati Enquirer*, Oct. 5, 1997.

Mark A. Norell, Eugene S. Gaffney, and Lowell Dingus, *Discovering Dinosaurs in the American Museum of Natural History* (New York: Alfred A. Knopf, Inc., 1995), p. 190.

David Norman, *The Illustrated Encyclopedia of Dinosaurs* (London: Salamander Books Ltd., 1985), p. 70.

Mary Schweitzer and Tracy Staedter, "The Real Jurassic Park," *Earth*, June 1997, p. 55–57.

Sothebys, Sue: *The Tyrannosaurus Rex,* 1997. http://www.sothebys.com/sue_trex/ homejs.html

The Dragon

Michael Benton, *Dinosaurs: An A-Z Guide* (New York: Derrydale Books, 1988), p. 34.

Philip J. Currie and Kevin Padian, editors, *Encyclopedia of Dinosaurs*, "European Dinosaurs," by Eric Buffetaut (San Diego, CA: Academic Press, 1997), p. 212–216.

Dougal Dixon, Barry Cox, R.J.G. Savage, and Brian Gardiner, *The MacMillan Illustrated Encyclopedia of Dinosaurs and Prehistoric Animals* (New York: Macmillan Publishing Co., 1988), p. 113.

Tim Gardom and Angela Milner, *The Book of Dinosaurs: The Natural History Museum Guide* (Rocklin, CA: Prima Publishing, 1993), p. 104–118.

David Lambert, *The Ultimate Dinosaur Book* (Kindersley, London: Dorling Kindersley, 1993), p. 58–59.

Philip J. Currie and Kevin Padian, *Encyclopedia of Dinosaurs*, "Spinosauridae and Baronychidae," by Angela Milner (San Diego, CA: Academic Press, 1997), p. 699–700.

Philip J. Currie and Kevin Padian, *Encyclopedia of Dinosaurs*, "Teeth and Jaws," by P. Martin Sander (San Diego, CA: Academic Press, 1997), p. 717–725.

Philip J. Currie and Kevin Padian, *Encyclopedia of Dinosaurs*, "Ornamentation," by Matthew K. Vickaryous and Michael J. Ryan (San Diego, CA: Academic Press, 1997), p. 488–493.

Plesiosaur

Michael Benton, *Dinosaur and Other Prehistoric Animal Fact Finder* (New York: Kingfisher Books, 1992), p. 77.

Dougal Dixon, Barry Cox, R.J.G. Savage, and Brian Gardiner, *The MacMillan Illustrated Encyclopedia of Dinosaurs and Prehistoric Animals* (New York: Macmillan Publishing Co., 1988), p. 76–77.

Mark A. Norell, Eugene S. Gaffney, and Lowell Dingus, *Discovering Dinosaurs in the American Museum of Natural History* (New York: Alfred A. Knopf, Inc., 1995), p. 57–59.

David Norman, *The Illustrated Encyclopedia of Dinosaurs* (London: Salamander Books Ltd., 1985), p. 178–179.

Joseph Wallace, *Book of Dinosaurs and Other Ancient Creatures* (New York: Simon & Schuster, 1994), p. 131.

Leviathan

Jack M. Callaway and Elizabeth L. Nicholls, editors, Anicent Marine Reptiles, "Morphological Constraints on Tetrapod Feeding Mechanisms: Why Were There No Suspension-Feeding Marine Reptiles," by Rachel Collin and Christine M. Janis (San Diego, CA: Academic Press, 1997), p. 464.

Sylvia J. Czerkas and Stephen A. Czerkas, *Dinosaurs: A Global View* (New York: Barnes & Noble Books, 1996), p. 179, 182.

Dougal Dixon, Barry Cox, R.J.G. Savage, and Brian Gardiner, *The MacMillan Illustrated Encyclopedia of Dinosaurs and Prehistoric Animals* (New York: Macmillan Publishing Co., 1988), p. 77.

"Kronosaurus queenslandicus, Australia's Marine Giant," *The Gondwana Gazette*, 1997, http://easyweb,firmware.com.au/firebird/page5.htm

David Norman, *The Illustrated Encyclopedia of Dinosaurs* (London: Salamander Books Ltd., 1985), p. 179.

Pteranodon

Sylvia J. Czerkas and Stephen A. Czerkas, *Dinosaurs: A Global View* (New York: Barnes & Noble Books, 1996), p. 220.

Dougal Dixon, Barry Cox, R.J.G. Savage, and Brian Gardiner, *The MacMillan Illustrated Encyclopedia of Dinosaurs and Prehistoric Animals* (New York: Macmillan Publishing Co., 1988), p. 104–105.

David Norman, *The Illustrated Encyclopedia of Dinosaurs* (London: Salamander Books Ltd., 1985), p. 170–173.

Joseph Wallace, *Book of Dinosaurs and Other Ancient Creatures* (New York: Simon & Schuster, 1994), p. 138–139.

Peter Wellnhofer, *The Illustrated Encyclopedia of Prehistoric Flying Reptiles* (New York: Barnes & Noble Books, 1991), p. 136–145.

Stegosaurus

Michael Benton, *Dinosaurs: An A-Z Guide* (New York: Derrydale Books, 1988), p. 146, 166–168.

Philip J. Currie and Kevin Padian, *Encyclopedia of Dinosaurs*, "Skin," by Stephen A. Czerkas (San Diego, CA: Academic Press, 1997), p. 669–675.

Dougal Dixon, Barry Cox, R.J.G. Savage, and Brian Gardiner, *The MacMillan Illustrated Encyclopedia of Dinosaurs and Prehistoric Animals* (New York: Macmillan Publishing Co., 1988), p. 156.

Philip J. Currie and Kevin Padian, *Encyclopedia of Dinosaurs*, "Stegosauria," by Peter M. Galton (San Diego, CA: Academic Press, 1997), p. 701–703.

Tim Gardom and Angela Milner, *The Book of Dinosaurs: The Natural History Museum Guide* (Rocklin, CA: Prima Publishing, 1993), p. 123.

Mark A. Norell, Eugene S. Gaffney, and Lowell Dingus, *Discovering Dinosaurs in the American Museum of Natural History* (New York: Alfred A. Knopf, Inc., 1995), p. 146–148.

David Norman, *The Illustrated Encyclopedia of Dinosaurs* (London: Salamander Books Ltd., 1985), p. 152–157.

Philip J. Currie and Kevin Padian, *Encyclopedia of Dinosaurs*, "Ornithischia," by Kevin Padian (San Diego, CA: Academic Press, 1997), p. 494–498.

Philip J. Currie and Kevin Padian, *Encyclopedia of Dinosaurs*, "Intelligence," by Dale A. Russell (San Diego, CA: Academic Press, 1997), p. 370–372.

Philip J. Currie and Kevin Padian, *Encyclopedia of Dinosaurs*, "Ornamentation," by Matthew K. Vickaryous and Michael J. Ryan (San Diego, CA: Academic Press, 1997), p. 488–493.

Joseph Wallace, *Book of Dinosaurs and Other Ancient Creatures* (New York: Simon & Schuster, 1994), p. 107.

Behemoth

Philip J. Currie and Kevin Padian, *Encyclopedia of Dinosaurs*, "Biomechanics," by R. McNeill Alexander (San Diego, CA: Academic Press, 1997), p. 57–59.

Philip J. Currie and Kevin Padian, *Encyclopedia of Dinosaurs*, "Size and Scaling," by R. McNeill Alexander (San Diego, CA: Academic Press, 1997), p. 665–667.

Michael Benton, *Dinosaurs: An A-Z Guide* (New York: Derrydale Books, 1988), p. 35, 166–168.

Dougal Dixon, Barry Cox, R.J.G. Savage, and Brian Gardiner, *The MacMillan Illustrated Encyclopedia of Dinosaurs and Prehistoric Animals* (New York: Macmillan Publishing Co., 1988), p. 128–129.

Philip J. Currie and Kevin Padian, *Encyclopedia of Dinosaurs*, "Long Necks of Sauropods," by Eberhard Frey and John Martin (San Diego, CA: Academic Press, 1997), p. 406–409.

Tim Gardom and Angela Milner, *The Book of Dinosaurs: The Natural History Museum Guide* (Rocklin, CA: Prima Publishing, 1993), p. 118.

Philip J. Currie and Kevin Padian, *Encyclopedia of Dinosaurs*, "Tendaguru," by Gerhard Maier (San Diego, CA: Academic Press, 1997), p. 725–726.

Philip J. Currie and Kevin Padian, *Encyclopedia of Dinosaurs*, "Sauropoda," by John S. McIntosh (San Diego, CA: Academic Press, 1997), p. 654–658.

Triceratops
Philip J. Currie and Kevin Padian, *Encyclopedia of Dinosaurs*, "Size and Scaling," by R. McNeill Alexander (San Diego, CA: Academic Press, 1997), p. 665–667.

Michael Benton, *Dinosaurs: An A-Z Guide* (New York: Derrydale Books, 1988), p. 159, 166–168.

Philip J. Currie and Kevin Padian, *Encyclopedia of Dinosaurs*, "Hindlimbs and Feet," by Per Christiansen (San Diego, CA: Academic Press, 1997), p. 320–328.

Philip J. Currie and Kevin Padian, *Encyclopedia of Dinosaurs*, "Skin," by Stephen A. Czerkas (San Diego, CA: Academic Press, 1997), p. 669–675.

Dougal Dixon, Barry Cox, R.J.G. Savage, and Brian Gardiner, *The MacMillan Illustrated Encyclopedia of Dinosaurs and Prehistoric Animals* (New York: Macmillan Publishing Co., 1988), p. 164–168.

Philip J. Currie and Kevin Padian, *Encyclopedia of Dinosaurs*, "American Dinosaurs," by Peter Dodson (San Diego, CA: Academic Press, 1997), p. 10–13.

Philip J. Currie and Kevin Padian, *Encyclopedia of Dinosaurs*, "Neoceratopsia," by Peter Dodson (San Diego, CA: Academic Press, 1997), p. 473–478.

Philip J. Currie and Kevin Padian, *Encyclopedia of Dinosaurs*, "Paleoecology," by Peter Dodson (San Diego, CA: Academic Press, 1997), p. 515–519.

Philip J. Currie and Kevin Padian, *Encyclopedia of Dinosaurs*, "Edmonton Group," by David A. Eberth (San Diego, CA: Academic Press, 1997), p. 199–204.

Tim Gardom and Angela Milner, *The Book of Dinosaurs: The Natural History Museum Guide* (Rocklin, CA: Prima Publishing, 1993), p. 123.

Mark A. Norell, Eugene S. Gaffney, and Lowell Dingus, *Discovering Dinosaurs in the American Museum of Natural History* (New York: Alfred A. Knopf, Inc., 1995), p. 172–173.

David Norman, *The Illustrated Encyclopedia of Dinosaurs* (London: Salamander Books Ltd., 1985), p. 138–139, 200–201.

Philip J. Currie and Kevin Padian, *Encyclopedia of Dinosaurs*, "Diet," by Michael J. Ryan and Matthew K. Vickaryous (San Diego, CA: Academic Press, 1997), p. 169–174.

Joseph Wallace, *Book of Dinosaurs and Other Ancient Creatures* (New York: Simon & Schuster, 1994), p. 109.

FOR FURTHER INFORMATION

Answers in Genesis ministries are evangelical, Christ-centered, non-denominational, and non-profit.

Answers in Genesis
P.O. Box 6330
Florence, KY 41022
USA

Answers in Genesis
P.O. Box 39005
Howick, Auckland
New Zealand

Answers in Genesis
P.O. Box 6302
Acacia Ridge DC
QLD 4110
Australia

Answers in Genesis
P.O. Box 5262
Leicester LE2 3XU
United Kingdom

Answers in Genesis
5-420 Erb St. West
Suite 213
Waterloo, Ontario
Canada N2L 6K6

Answers in Genesis
Attn: Nao Hanada
3317-23 Nagaoka, Ibaraki-machi
Higashi-ibaraki-gun,
Ibaraki-ken 311-3116
Japan

In addition, you may contact:

Institute for Creation Research
P.O. Box 2667
El Cajon, CA 92021

If you want more faith-building ANSWERS, or for further information on dinosaurs and a wide variety of creation/evolution hot topics, free transparency masters, questions and answers, newsletters, *Creation ex nihilo* magazine and *Creation ex nihilo Technical Journal* information and more, check out our Website at:
www.AnswersinGenesis.org

ILLUSTRATOR/PHOTO CREDITS

All illustrations by: Dan Lietha

Triceratops skull, page 162: Black Hills Geological Institute

T. Rex skull ("Stan"), page 24: Restored and molded by Peter   Larson from BHGI

Hadrosaur skull, page 116: Re-restored by Joe Taylor from Mt. Blanco Collection (originally found in the Lance Creek Formation, circa 1910)

Trilobite, page 107: Tucson dealer, found in the Anti/Atlas mountains of Morocco

Tylosaur skeleton, page 42: Molded by Mike Triebold of Triebold Paleontology

Tylosaur skull, page 137: Molded by Mike Triebold of Triebold Paleontology

Corythosaurus skeleton, page 138: Photographed by Len Morris

Large *Carnosaur* Skeleton, page 52: Photographed by Ken Ham

Protoceratops skull, page 64: Photographed by Stewart Larson

Protoceratops andresnsi eggs, page 59: Photographed by Stewart Larson

Foot of *Saurolophus*, page 68: Photographed by Stewart Larson

Photos by Dan Lietha, Sculptures by Buddy Davis

Pteranodon, page 48

Pachycephalosaurus, page 131

Chasmosaurus, page 136

Dilophosaurus, page 148

Protoceratops, page 151

Heterodontosaurus, page 154

THE AUTHOR

Since coming to America in 1987, Australian Ken Ham has already become one of the most in-demand Christian conference speakers in the United States. Each year he gives dozens of faith-building talks to tens of thousands of children and adults on such topics as dinosaurs, creation vs. evolution, and the reliability of the Bible, etc.

The founder and executive director of Answers in Genesis (a ministry begun in 1994 to defend the authority of the Bible from the very first verse), Ken is the author of many books on Genesis, including the best-selling *The Lie: Evolution*, and the children's rhyme book on dinosaurs, *D is for Dinosaur.*

Ken is heard daily on the radio program *Answers . . . with Ken Ham* (broadcast on 400 outlets worldwide), and is a frequent guest on nationwide talk shows.

Answers in Genesis will be building a large museum in the Cincinnati, Ohio, area, in which many large dinosaur models (some pictured in this book) — each exceptionally sculpted — will be displayed, as well as other world-class exhibits.

Ken and his wife, Mally, have five children and reside in the Cincinnati/Northern Kentucky area.

FOR FURTHER READING

THE LIE: EVOLUTION
Ken Ham

Humorous and easy to read, this book powerfully equips Christians to defend the Book of Genesis and opens eyes to the evil effects of evolution on today's society. 190 pages. (Junior High – Adult)
  ISBN: 0-89051-158-6 • $9.95

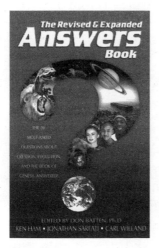

THE ANSWERS BOOK
Ken Ham, Jonathan Sarfati, and Carl Wieland

This fascinating book addresses the most common questions that Christians and non-Christians alike ask regarding creation/evolution and Genesis. The 12 most-asked questions, such as: Where did Cain get his wife? What about continental drift? Also, dinosaurs, the gap theory, carbon dating, origin of races, etc. are answered in an easy-to-understand manner (with helpful illustrations.) 288 pages. (High School – Adult)
  ISBN: 0-89051-161-6 • $11.99

AVAILABLE AT CHRISTIAN BOOKSTORES NATIONWIDE

ONE BLOOD
Ken Ham, Carl Wieland, and Don Batten

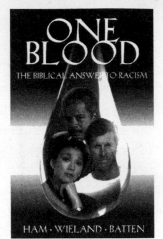

More than half a century has passed since the horrors of the Nazi racial extermination camps were revealed to a disbelieving world. Yet the battle of ethnic hate and violence remains one of the burning issues of our time. Billions of dollars are spent fighting it. Oprah devotes entire programs to it. Presidents consult civic and religious leaders; everyone seems to be wrestling with the problems of racial prejudice, yet solutions evade us. 176 pages. (High School – Adult)

ISBN: 0-89051-276-0 • $10.99

CREATION: FACTS OF LIFE
Gary Parker

Dr. Parker, a leading creation scientist and AiG speaker, presents the classic arguments for evolution used in public schools, universities, and the media, and refutes them in an entertaining and easy-to-read style. A must for students and teachers alike. This is a great book to give to a non-Christian as a witnessing tool. 216 pages. (High School – Adult)

ISBN: 0-89051-200-0 • $10.95

AVAILABLE AT CHRISTIAN BOOKSTORES NATIONWIDE

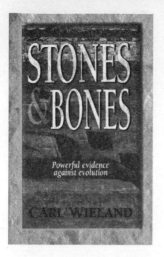

STONES AND BONES – POWERFUL EVIDENCE AGAINST EVOLUTION
Carl Wieland

Basic reasons why Christians (and some non-Christians) reject evolution in favor of creation. Easy-to-understand explanations on fossils, "missing links," mutations, dinosaurs, natural selection, and more. 48 pages. (Ages 13 – Adult)
ISBN: 0-89051-175-6 • $2.95

THE YOUNG EARTH
John D. Morris

Dr. John Morris, a geologist, explains in easy-to-understand terms how true science supports a young earth. Includes a critique of major dating methods. Filled with facts that will equip layman and scientists alike. Transparency masters are provided in the second half of this book. Use them in your Sunday school, church, or youth group to challenge and teach. 208 pages. (High School – Adult)

ISBN: 0-89051-174-8 • $14.95